# How to Sell
# COMPUTERS AND ACCESSORIES
## on
# eBay

Other Entrepreneur Pocket Guides include
*How to Sell Clothing, Shoes, and Accessories on eBay*
*How to Sell Collectibles on eBay*
*How to Sell Toys and Hobbies on eBay*
*Start Your Real Estate Career*
*Start Your Restaurant Career*

**Entrepreneur Magazine's Pocket Guides**

# How to Sell
# COMPUTERS AND ACCESSORIES
# on eBay

*Entrepreneur Press and
J. S. McDougall*

**Ep
Entrepreneur
Press**

Editorial Director: Jere L. Calmes
Cover Design: Beth Hansen-Winter
Production and Composition: Eliot House Productions

© 2006 by Entrepreneur Media Inc.
All rights reserved.
Reproduction or translation of any part of this work beyond that permitted by Section 107 or 108 of the 1976 United States Copyright Act without permission of the copyright owner is unlawful. Requests for permission or further information should be addressed to the Business Products Division, Entrepreneur Media Inc.

This publication is designed to provide accurate and authoritative information in regard to the subject matter covered. It is sold with the understanding that the publisher is not engaged in rendering legal, accounting or other professional services. If legal advice or other expert assistance is required, the services of a competent professional person should be sought.

**Library of Congress Cataloging-in-Publication**
McDougall, J. S.
   How to sell computers and accessories on eBay/by Entrepreneur Press and J.S. McDougall.
    p.   cm.
   ISBN 1-59918-044-8 (alk. paper)
   1. Selling—Computers. 2. eBay (Firm) 3. Internet auctions. I. Entrepreneur Press. II. Title.
HF5439.C67M35 2006
621.39068'8—dc22                       2006022187

Printed in Canada
12 11 10 09 08 07 06                        10 9 8 7 6 5 4 3 2 1

# Contents

Preface . . . . . . . . . . . . . . . . . . . . . . . . . . . . . . . . . . . xi

*Chapter 1*
## Selling Computers and Accessories . . . . . . . . . . . 1
PowerSelling versus Selling as a Hobby . . . . . . . . . . . . . . 2
Competition. . . . . . . . . . . . . . . . . . . . . . . . . . . . . . . . . . . 3
Brick-and-Mortar Competition. . . . . . . . . . . . . . . . . . . . . . 4
Online Competition . . . . . . . . . . . . . . . . . . . . . . . . . . . . . 7
The Tech-Trickle-Down . . . . . . . . . . . . . . . . . . . . . . . . . . 9

*Chapter 2*
## The PowerSellers . . . . . . . . . . . . . . . . . . . . . . . . . 11

## Chapter 3
### The Logistics................................17
Enter Your Information........................... 18
Account Setup ................................. 21
My eBay ....................................... 25

## Chapter 4
### Inventory Resources ........................27
New Items...................................... 28
Used Items .................................... 32
Buy Smart...................................... 35

## Chapter 5
### Listing Items ...............................37
Auctions ...................................... 37
Categories..................................... 38
Title and Description .......................... 41
Pricing and Duration ........................... 43
Quantity....................................... 47
Payment Methods................................ 52
Ship-To Locations.............................. 53
Shipping and Sales Tax......................... 54
Sales Tax...................................... 55
Return Policy.................................. 55
Payment Instructions........................... 55
Review and Submit.............................. 55
eBay Stores.................................... 56

## Chapter 6
## Pricing .................................. 61
Starting Price................................. 62

## Chapter 7
## Selling Your Items ......................... 69
The Title ....................................... 70
Description ..................................... 71
Make Your Pictures Worth
  More Than 1,000 Words ....................... 73

## Chapter 8
## Customer Care ............................. 77
Pre-Auction ..................................... 77
During Auctions................................. 78
Post-Auction .................................... 80
When Things Go Wrong .......................... 81
Beware of Scams ................................ 82
Conflict Resolution.............................. 83

## Chapter 9
## Starting a Business........................ 85
Finances ....................................... 85
Business Types ................................. 87
Registering Your Business Name.................. 89
Inventory Issues................................ 90

*Chapter 10*
## Tools to Help You Work Smarter ............ 93
Research Tools ................................ 94
Auction Management Tools ...................... 97
Photo Hosting Services ........................ 99

*Chapter 11*
## Advanced Marketing Strategies. ............ 103
Marketing within eBay ......................... 104
Marketing Outside eBay ........................ 108

*Chapter 12*
## Inventory Management. .................... 111
Drop-Shipping ................................. 111
Taking on Inventory ........................... 113
Shipping ...................................... 117

*Chapter 13*
## Finances ................................. 119
Doing It Yourself ............................. 120
Business Vital Signs .......................... 121
Finding Help .................................. 123

*Chapter 14*
## Human Resources ......................... 125
When to Hire .................................. 126
Before You Hire ............................... 126

After You Hire ................................ 129

*Chapter 15*
**Final Thoughts** ........................... 133
　Closing Thoughts from PowerSellers ................ 134

**Index** ...................................... 137

# Preface

The story is common. It's 10 P.M. on a Monday night. You're trapped in a company-wide corporate training session listening to a lecture on the virtues of TPS reports and "positive and specific corrective feedback." You chair is uncomfortable, your stomach is empty, and you're faced with the horror of repeating this every day for a week. While staring at the flickering fluorescent lights, you are struck with two thoughts: throwing your shoe at the speaker is probably not a good idea, and the time has finally come to start your own business. You throw your shoe, and leave.

If this story sounds familiar, you're in good company. Throngs of people, just like you, are searching for, and finding, better ways to make ends meet, earn extra cash, and maybe even strike it rich. Advances in internet technology makes it possible for Lil' ol' You to instantly connect with millions of people. If you have a good idea for a business and a solid plan for growth, there's no limit to how large—and profitable—your idea can become.

Setting up on the internet with your own web site presents many advantages: your products are immediately available to anyone with an internet connection; e-promotion can be cheap and efficient; and automated payment processing simplifies finances. However, running your own web site is not without its own set of challenges: building web site traffic can be complicated; strict security measures must be taken to protect customers; and maintaining a large web site is, in itself, a full-time job.

Luckily for us, eBay has addressed many of these challenges. eBay provides the web site, the payment processing, and the rigorous marketing. And eBay provides over 100 million potential customers right to your virtual doorstep. For these reasons, and many more, eBay is a great place to start your business.

eBay was developed by Pierre Omidyar in 1995 with the idea that it would be an internet site to help individuals buy and sell items online. But, after product resellers, retailers, and manufacturers learned of eBay's many virtues, it quickly grew to become the world's marketplace that it is today. More than 100 million people are currently a part of the eBay community and over 1 billion items are sold on eBay every year. Though the market potential is staggering, the task of grabbing the attention of, and then successfully selling to, that market is not easily accomplished. You will have many competitors and obstacles, along the road to becoming a PowerSeller. This book will provide the tools necessary to begin selling computers and computer accessories at a rate you never thought possible while sitting in those corporate training sessions taking aim with your shoe.

*For Caroline,
my inspiration and courage.*

CHAPTER 1

# Selling Computers
# and Accessories

COMPUTERS AND COMPUTER ACCESSORIES ARE SOME OF the best-selling and most reliably profitable items on eBay. Thousands of people visit eBay every day to browse and shop for new PCs, printers, networking components, cables, monitors, and many other computer-related items. Many savvy eBay sellers have already recognized and capitalized on eBay's large and hungry market for everything computer related. With some research, foresight, and careful planning, you can join their ranks.

Though selling on eBay is a great way to earn money, it is not a get-rich-quick miracle. Care must be taken when conducting all your transactions and dealing with bidders. eBay's feedback system is a double-edged sword. It will, at once, boast to the world how great a seller you are, while revealing to the world exactly where you are lagging behind. It takes a lot of work to make and keep buyers happy. If you've ever had a job that deals directly with the public, then you know this already. If you do not have the time or interest to devote to taking care of the details of doing business, such as getting packages to the shipping store on time in the middle of a snowstorm, or answering buyer e-mails after a long day of crunching numbers in your cubicle, then selling on eBay is not for you. Your feedback score will suffer, and soon buyers will shy away from your listings. However, if you're ready and excited for the possibilities eBay presents, then you will have a rewarding and profitable experience.

## PowerSelling versus Selling as a Hobby

The first step in selling on eBay is to decide your commitment level to this endeavor. There are two levels of commitment when discussing selling on eBay: hobby seller and PowerSeller. The hobby seller sells casually for extra cash when she finds time in her schedule. The PowerSeller has made selling online her career. The tips found in this book will help both the hobby seller and PowerSeller become more successful, but the initial planning for these two commitment levels is decidedly different. We'll discuss the differences throughout the book, but for now just think carefully about whether you want to depend on selling computers on eBay as your only income, or if you'd like for it to supplement what you're already earning elsewhere.

Both hobby selling and PowerSelling can be fun, exciting, and lucrative. If you're not sure where to begin, plan to start small and grow over time. It's much easier to start selling as a hobby to supplement your job than it is to start selling full time and then grovel for your job back if you decide this career isn't for you.

## Competition

Of all the possible items to sell, selling computers is a smart choice. Technology is growing and evolving at such a rapid rate that there is near constant demand for more products. However, because these items are immensely popular with bidders, they are also immensely popular with eBay sellers—which means that you will find plenty of competition in this category. Be aware that if you plan to reach the coveted PowerSeller status, you have your work cut out for you. Many PowerSellers are busy not only keeping a careful eye on their own businesses, but they also have learned to keep a strict eye on their competition—you.

The bright side of having a lot of competition is that it provides a lot of opportunities for market research. This is where we begin your journey to becoming a successful eBay computer seller. Know your competition, both on eBay and off. What are their strengths? More importantly, what are their weaknesses? If your competition sells on eBay, find and study their product listings. Are they attractive, complete, and clear? Read their customer feedback comments. Are buyers complaining about slow shipping, inaccurate descriptions, or poor customer service? Find these faults, and make it your goal to provide better service in these areas.

To help you get a jump on researching the companies that you'll be competing with, we've compiled a list of the most prominent. We'll begin with your non-eBay competition. Go to the web sites of these sellers and read their shipping and returns policies and find online reviews. Do everything you can to get a sense of what their customers like and dislike about their businesses. Make note of what you find and incorporate your findings into the beginnings of your business plan.

## Brick-and-Mortar Competition

When selling items on eBay, you not only have other eBay sellers to contend with, but you are still competing with actual stores. The following will help you position your products as professionally as your brick-and-mortar competition.

### BestBuy (www.bestbuy.com)

BestBuy focuses not only on computers, but on all sorts of technology and appliances. They sell everything from gas-range stoves to iPods to monitors. BestBuy can offer customers one main experience that you cannot by selling on eBay—the in-store fondling experience. Buyers that walk into BestBuy can pick up, twist, turn, and physically handle everything they wish to buy. This experience helps the buyer to know exactly what the item will look like sitting on her desk at home. Your job is to try to replicate this experience as closely as possible in your product descriptions by using scores of photos, listing precise dimensions, and by writing accurate and compelling descriptions of every feature and flaw on the item.

## Wal-Mart (www.walmart.com)

Most people do not see Wal-Mart as a computer seller. Sure they have clothing, shampoo, bicycles, and frozen peas, but they also boast a little computer corner tucked away behind the DVDs. While the store itself is nearly ubiquitous in American towns, their selection of computer systems and components is quite limited. They sell mostly low-end Compaq and HP computer systems, with some shelves devoted to networking equipment and USB peripherals. Believe it or not, with the aid of eBay, you can compete with Wal-Mart by offering a larger selection of quality computers and high-end items for niche markets, such as laser printers, CPUs, or logic boards.

## CompUSA (www.compusa.com)

CompUSA is your closest competitor item-wise. Everything they sell is included in the scope of this book. They have stores across the country, offer customers the ability to touch and feel items, and have a fully-stocked online store. So how can you compete with a company so large that deals directly in your market? Beat them with customer service and product expertise. Your passion for computers will serve you well here, and will no doubt put you ahead of any low-wage retail employee watching the clock waiting for his shift to end. When dealing with buyers, be excited about your products, helpful to their needs, and happy to help them with anything they ask. Before long, you'll have a long line of repeat customers that see you as their source for their computer products and information.

### Apple Computer (www.apple.com)

Until a few years ago, Apple would not have qualified as a brick-and-mortar competitor. But due to their recent push into upscale shopping malls across the world, they are becoming a huge retail computer force. These Apple stores offer quality customer service, a pleasing shopping atmosphere, the hot gadgets of the day, and an unbeatable touch-and-feel experience. Luckily for you, Apple computers can be expensive. And therefore, after some supplier research, you will find it easy to compete with Apple on price with comparable non-Apple products.

### Local Computer Shops

Most towns have a small locally-owned computer store tucked away on the second floor of the building behind the post office. This store will likely provide customers with great customer service, decent selection, and instant gratification. But they likely also only see a few customers per day. eBay's millions of buyers and constant traffic can put more customers into your store in an hour than these small shops will see all week. The key to success will be learning how to capture that eBay traffic.

## Online Competition

You are likely to find that researching online stores is much easier than their brick-and-mortar counterparts. To fill the need for customer reassurance when conducting transactions online, hundreds of customer-review sites have popped up across the internet. Search on Google for reviews of any computer retailers and you'll be pleasantly surprised to find many independent sites with customer reviews and comments.

### newegg.com

Newegg.com is a great business with a funny name. The items they sell will be directly competing with your items. They cater to casual computer shoppers, power users, gamers, the build-your-own niche, and everyone in between. For each item they sell, they have extensive customer reviews, impressive photo galleries, and detailed descriptions and technical information. They do a good job of recreating the touch-and-feel experience that their brick-and-mortar competitors offer.

And, if that weren't enough, they provide fast and reasonably priced shipping. Newegg.com is a business to emulate.

## *tigerdirect.com*

TigerDirect has a catalog similar to the newegg.com catalog. They sell most anything that you would aim to sell, so in that way, they are direct competition. But they are a retailer, and therefore buyers will likely search eBay first to see if they can find a particular item cheaper. If you have found the right supplier, automated the bulk of your business, and use a reliable shipping company, chances are you can provide the item for less than a retail company due to your lower overall overhead. If you find yourself unable to beat companies such as TigerDirect on price, you can always compete with them through great customer service.

## *apple.com*

Apple, as mentioned earlier, does a large percentage of its business through its web site. Study the thoroughness of Apple's product descriptions. Take note of the great lengths they take to recreate the customer's in-store experience. These tactics will serve you well too.

## *alienware.com*

Alienware caters to the gamer niche. They build and sell high-end performance systems in elaborate cases with all the gadgets and doodads that gamers want. They are known for quality hardware and high prices. If you're looking to compete in the gamer market, try to build or buy computer systems that have quality components but can be sold profitably for less. Research your customers. Find out what is most important to them, and make sure to deliver it. You might try to save money by packaging these components in less ornate computer cases.

You'll find when researching your competition that buyers have countless options for where to buy their computers and computer accessories. It is often impossible to compete with all these sellers on price alone. There are sure to be larger sellers out there who can buy in such large bulk quantities that their per-item price drops significantly. One day, you will be able to do the same, but when you're starting out, you should focus on competing on customer service, attractive and complete eBay listings, and reliable shipping. You will soon build a feedback score that will attract the buyers you need to begin buying and selling items on par with the PowerSellers. Before you know it, you'll be a PowerSeller yourself.

## The Tech-Trickle-Down

The computer market is still in its infancy. New, or first-generation, technology is being introduced nearly every day. Companies like Apple, Intel, and Sony are redefining the "cutting-edge" with seemingly every press conference they hold. This rapid development rate of new technologies and the premium price on those new technologies create a trickle-down effect. Large companies and power users buy the first-generation technology as soon as it becomes available to the public. This technology could be anything from new CPUs to faster hard drives to biometric scanners. Upon introduction, these new items fetch too high a price for the average user to buy and therefore comprise a limited segment of the market. But, inevitably, new technology is introduced that improves upon, and replaces, the previously latest and greatest technology, making it the new second generation. This second-generation equipment is now cheaper and more accessible to the average user. So the number of units sold actually increases to fill the large demand created by buyers who waited for the price to come down. Then, when new technologies are again introduced, this now third generation equipment is moved down the chain to users who don't mind, or are oblivious to, old hardware. Think of third-generation hardware as the old ThinkPad sitting on your mother's desk, or grandpop's Apple IIe.

You have an opportunity to sell at every step in the technology trickle-down process. Pre-order new technology before launch to capitalize on the high, post-launch demand. Watch the hot technology companies to find out when they are set to launch a new product and buy up the inventories of retailers selling off soon-to-be second-generation equipment to make room for the new first generation. Finally, sell off third-generation items at high-volume and rock-bottom prices to turn a profit. Seek new markets for old hardware, such as collectors, hobbyists, and young businesses.

CHAPTER 2

# The PowerSellers

*T*O HELP BRING TO LIGHT THE OPPORTUNITIES AND obstacles of selling computers on eBay, we have interviewed some top sellers in the Computers & Networking category. Each of the sellers profiled below has attained PowerSeller status. To become a PowerSeller, a seller must:

- Have been an active seller on eBay for more than 90 days
- List at least four items per month for the last three months
- Reached a feedback level of at least 100 with a 98 percent positive rating
- Generate at least $1,000 per month for at least three months in a row

As you can see, PowerSellers have found a strategy that works! And the PowerSellers in this book have been gracious enough to share their time and knowledge with us. Below is a brief description of each PowerSeller and his or her business. You will also find helpful tips from these sellers in the chapters ahead.

### *notebooksauction-dot-com*

Benjamin Scott, who started his eBay business with a partner in 1999, had been researching and purchasing a lot of laptops on eBay for their general use and hobby when it occurred to them that it might be conceivable to buy computer lots on eBay, refurbish what they could, and resell them. They started buying up used computers on eBay and a few other auction sites that existed at the time.

Today, they continue to buy and sell laptops from their warehouse and shop in Pennsylvania. By buying up end-of-lease laptops from various suppliers, they are able to maintain a steady inventory source of two- to three-year-old Dell laptops. This inventory is then spread among their eBay auctions, eBay Store, external web site, and they even supply several computer shops around their area.

Ben and his partner must be doing something right. In just a few years, the company has grown to employ six full-time workers, attain eBay's PowerSeller status, and achieved a 99.7 percent positive feedback rating of 3,489. This is a business to watch.

## somersetsales

Mark Nicotera, the owner of Somerset Capital Group Ltd., began selling on eBay in 2001. He does not operate his company solely as an eBay business, like many PowerSellers. Rather, he uses eBay as a sales channel to offload some of the returns from his main business of leasing technology to corporate clients. Somerset sells primarily laptop computers and Apple computer products on eBay, but also offer items such as monitors and projectors.

Mark has five employees who devote part of their day to handling the company's eBay auctions. The rest of their time is spent managing the over $500 million worth of leased technology that the company owns all over North America. When the leases on their equipment expire and their assets are returned to them, Somerset Capital is able to sell the equipment through established customer relationships, leasing equipment remarketers, and, of course, eBay. Selling on eBay, Mark says, allows them to receive a higher price on some items than they would receive through their traditional brokers.

Somerset Capital, somersetsales on eBay, has earned a 99.7 percent positive feedback rating from its eBay buyers. Mark hopes to expand his company's sales on eBay in the future and is considering the possibility of purchasing equipment solely to sell on eBay. With his steady inventory source, his high positive feedback, and his vast knowledge of the items he's selling, we'd say Mark has a good chance of meeting those goals.

## chessmasterjack

John Kreutzer is a Mac-fanatic. His history of using, fixing, and teaching Apple computers dates back to their very first models in the late 1970s. In 2001, John decided to capitalize on his expertise by starting a business buying and selling his favorite computers. But you won't find only computers in his eBay Store, Jack's Mac Shop. You'll also find the Macintosh operating system, Apple's various applications, and all sorts of Apple computer peripherals.

The items he sells range from brand new to over 25 years old. John enjoys finding his Macs new homes with collectors, bargain hunters, and other Mac-fanatics. One of the parts of the business that he enjoys most, John says, is working with his customers to help them find the right products and solve any problems that emerge. Owning this business allows John to work with the products and systems that he finds exciting.

John's customers respond well to his enthusiasm for his products. They have awarded him a 99.6 percent positive feedback rating of 3,803. He is credited with being a fast shipper, very helpful during transactions, and having a profound grasp of all Apple and Apple-related products. John is a good example of creating a successful business out of doing what you love.

## goodasnewcomputers_canada

Anthony Barton and his company, Good As New Computers, have been selling used computers since 1998. When they opened, they were just a small shop in the Toronto area that sold end-of-lease computers from their parent company to walk-in customers. In 2003, when they noticed their sales lagging a bit, they turned to the internet as a way to boost revenue. John and his partners read some online guides, did some research, and finally decided that the best plan was to open up an eBay Store: Good As New Computers Canada.

Their parent company, Vernon Technology Solutions, keeps them in good supply of two- to three-year-old computers to sell. Though this inventory source maintains a steady stream of sales, they found that the demand on eBay could stand even more. So, to meet demand, they expanded their business by buying three- to five-year-old computers from various wholesalers to add to their sales inventory. Anthony now employs two full-time eBay sales people, a full-time technician for testing and configuring orders, and a full-time shipping manager. They also continue to sell through their retail outlet in Toronto, but eBay now makes up the bulk of their business.

Anthony and company ship items to happy customers all over North America. The computers, monitors, projectors, and parts that they sell receive excellent reviews every day. They are applauded for their excellent customer care and fast shipping practices. The company has earned a 99.2 percent positive feedback rating of 2,270, with over 1,000 of those transactions taking place within the last 12 months. Not too bad for what was once a small computer shop in Toronto.

## *mcpricebreakers*

Jeff, of MC Price Breakers, began selling on eBay in 1997. At first, like many others, he placed a few random items up to test the eBay waters. He quickly realized that this "little web site that could" would become a lucrative avenue for sales. Jeff was lucky to have preexisting relationships with computer parts suppliers and long-time computer business friends. That made it an easy decision for his company to start selling computer parts. Also, it didn't hurt that, as Jeff puts simply, "We like the computer parts business."

MC Price Breakers SCSI Store 'n More now boasts over 2,500 items, including computer cases, SCSI cables, adapters, USB and FireWire peripherals, and some Macintosh-compatible products. The overwhelming bulk of their business comes through their eBay Store where prices are fixed because they run the same auctions for popular items every week, which attracts attention and drives bidders to their store.

MC Price Breakers excels in customer feedback. Not only is it overwhelmingly positive at 99.9 percent, but they've managed to achieve that rating over the course of an astounding 15,123 transactions. In fact, they've only received 16 negative feedbacks from customers in nine years. Now that's a happy customer base. We applaud their customer service.

CHAPTER 3

# The Logistics

*R*EGISTERING FOR AN EBAY ACCOUNT IS PAINLESS. eBay has done a great job making the process straightforward. And while it may be technically easy, there are some steps that require careful consideration before submission.

To begin the process, click the Register link on eBay.com's main page. You will see a progress bar across the top of the page with the three steps in the registration process: Enter Information, Choose User ID & Password, and Check Your E-mail. You will also see a link for Live Help at the top of the page. Clicking this link will create a chat window that connects you with a member of the eBay customer service team. If you get stuck during this process or find yourself with a question, click this link for help.

## Enter Your Information
Enter your personal information into the appropriate text boxes on this page. Be sure to double check your information for accuracy, as this will be the information used to conduct business, and people need to trust that it is correct.

### User Agreement and Privacy Policy
Most people never take the time to read the User Agreements or Privacy Policies of the sites they join. In most cases, this practice in harmless. But in this case, we strongly suggest you read through eBay's User Agreement. It states, in no uncertain terms, the infractions that will get you kicked out of the eBay community, and banned from selling on the site. Not all of the infractions are obvious, and some make it quite conceivable that an unsuspecting new user could break one of them relatively easily. Realizing down the road that you have failed to abide by eBay's User Agreement can put an immediate end to your income. It has happened to unsuspecting sellers many times. Please read the User Agreement. Below are some forbidden actions that often trip up new users, with our comments.

While using the site, you will not:
- post content or items in an inappropriate category or areas on the site. (With something as simple as a missed

click of the mouse, a user could mistakenly post an item to an inappropriate category. Be sure to double-check.)
- manipulate the price of any item or interfere with other user's listings. (It is tempting and easy to bid on your own items to boost the sale price, but the practice is strictly forbidden.)
- distribute or post spam, chain letters, or pyramid schemes. (When the excitement of owning a new business strikes, many new users are tempted to contact as many people as possible to advertise their services. It may not seem so at the time, but this is spamming. It is not allowed through eBay's e-mail forms, in the discussion boards, or from any other contact information collected from eBay's site.)

eBay's User Agreement also contains a clear Content License clause, which states:

*When you give us content, you grant us a non-exclusive, worldwide, perpetual, irrevocable, royalty-free, sublicensable (through multiple tiers) right to exercise the copyright, publicity, and database rights (but no other rights) you have in the content, in any media known now or in the future. (We need these rights to host and display your content.)*

So, in other words, don't post the text of your upcoming novel as the description of an item, because once you do, eBay owns it. In addition to these points, there are several additional important facets of the User Agreement that should be known to every seller. Read it.

## Choose User ID and Password

Choosing the right User ID is important for all sellers. This User ID will be how people identify you and your business on eBay. Casual sellers have the luxury of considering a variation of their own name as a User ID, whereas more ambitious sellers do not. The User ID of your eBay business should be short, memorable, easily pronounced, and appropriate for your product line—while leaving room for later growth. For example, a seller of laser printers should choose a name that identifies the business as a seller of printing equipment, but doesn't rule out growth into selling ink jet, dot matrix, and thermal printers in the future. "LaserPrintTek" would be a poor choice, while "PrinterTek" will serve them better down the road. Also, more obviously, choose a User ID that is appropriate for the type of items you will be selling. "TeddyBearLuv" may be adorable but is misleading as a User ID for a seller of optical drives.

You may be asked to confirm your identity by entering a credit or debit card number. This is a safety measure to ensure you are over 18 years of age and have a valid mailing address. Your card will not be charged at this time.

## Check Your E-Mail

Once you have submitted all your information to eBay and select your User ID, you will be sent an e-mail asking you to confirm your registration. This e-mail will contain a confirmation code that you will need to enter into eBay's registration confirmation page. This e-mail and confirmation code validates that the e-mail address you entered is valid and that you have access to it. Follow the instructions in the confirmation e-mail and you will have completed your eBay registration.

Now, to begin selling you will need to register as a seller. Click the Start Selling link on the page that results from clicking the link in your registration confirmation e-mail. You will be asked to enter a credit or debit card number to place on file. This is, again, just a security measure to confirm your age, name, and address. You card will not be charged.

Next, you will be asked to input account and routing information for a checking account. This is a measure eBay takes to ensure that they will be able to collect the seller's fees if the credit or debit card you've provided expires. As the last step in this process you must select the method by which to pay your seller's fees: from the card you've just placed on file, or the bank account.

## Account Setup

Now that you're all set up with a seller account, the first order of business is to get your account set up with some necessary information. We will cover a few of the most important items here, but we can't cover everything, so it will be up to you to work your way down the options provided in the My Account menu on the left side of your My eBay page.

## Your "About Me" Page

The content of your "About Me" page is entirely up to you, and therefore gives you the opportunity to tell eBay buyers about yourself, your business, and your products. Most sellers use this page as a place to introduce themselves, put up some photos, lay out their shipping and payment policies, and perhaps link to a few of their auctions. If done well, your About Me page will show some personality, give buyers a sense of familiarity, and drive sales.

To begin setting up your About Me page, log in to your account, click Personal Information under the My Account menu on the left-hand side of the page. On the resulting page, you are able to edit all the personal information associated with your account. Click Edit next to the About Me page option.

There are two methods available for setting up an About Me page: through eBay's step-by-step process or by entering your own HTML code. Writing your own HTML code allows for more customization than the step-by-step process, but is only recommended for sellers who are comfortable writing HTML. This page is not a place where novice coders should cut their teeth. It must have a professional appearance to reflect your business well.

The step-by-step process will ask for a page title, some text, and some photographs. You can also display your recent sales history, and provide links to helpful web sites. This is the only page on which eBay will allow you to post off-eBay links, so do so wisely. Post links to web sites that will be helpful to your buyers. For example, posting a link to a CPU/Motherboard compatibility chart will help your buyers make a better purchasing decision, but posting a link to photos of your grandmother's lovable dog, Rapscallion, will not.

When writing the text for your About Me page you should consider including your business mailing address and telephone number. Buyers like to see that you are willing to provide real-world avenues for support. This is an easy way to immediately boost your buyers' confidence. However, if you work from home, and do not yet have a business mailing address and business-specific telephone line, you may not want to list your personal information. There's no limit to the amount of frustration one cranky customer armed with your home telephone number can cause. You should, however, prominently post an e-mail address at which to receive questions. Once you have inserted all your information and configured your options, you then select a layout, preview your page, and submit.

## *Selling Preferences*

From your My eBay page, click Preferences in the My Account menu. You will see a host of options that you should explore and set to your liking. In this preferences panel you are able to configure almost every facet of your eBay account, from which newsletters you receive to how you accept payments from buyers. This is also the first place you will be asked about PayPal.

## *PayPal*

PayPal enables people to send and receive money online. Having a PayPal account is similar to having a checking account at your local bank. You can deposit money to your PayPal account from your personal bank account, you can withdraw money from your PayPal account in various ways, including electronic transfer to your personal bank account, and you can send money from your PayPal account to any person with an e-mail address. PayPal made sending money online so easy that it quickly became the default method buyers used to pay for their eBay purchases. It became so widely used on eBay that in late 2002, eBay bought PayPal and began further integrating PayPal's services into its own.

Today, PayPal is ubiquitous among eBay auctions. Nearly every seller on eBay has a PayPal account at which they can receive payments from buyers. Not only does PayPal make sending money easier for buyers, it also provides sellers with the ability to accept instant payments, to accept major credit cards, and to avoid bounced checks and fraudulent money orders. It is not uncommon that only seconds after the end of an auction full payment has been delivered by the buyer to the seller's PayPal account—making the entire transaction easier for everyone.

One of the downsides of PayPal is that some buyers find it too risky a proposition to submit their sensitive financial information, such as bank account numbers and credit card information, when registering for a PayPal account. They, therefore, refuse to sign up for a PayPal account. For this reason, making your auctions "PayPal only" will alienate some potential buyers. You should be willing to accept other forms of payment from your buyers such as personal checks or money orders.

### Personal Checks and Money Orders

When accepting personal checks and money orders from buyers you should wait a few days to make sure the funds arrive in your account before making the shipment. Sometimes, whether intended by the buyer or not, personal checks will bounce, leaving you with the hassle of contacting the buyer and collecting payment. Also, a popular method of defrauding sellers on eBay is to send a counterfeit money order for the payment amount. You can and should protect yourself from these scams by waiting to ship any items. Make clear to buyers on each of your items' auction pages that if the buyer intends to use one of these two forms of payment that the shipping will be delayed while waiting for funds to clear.

## My eBay

The next step to setting up your eBay seller account is to familiarize yourself with your My eBay page. This screen will function as your eBay control panel. It provides up-to-the-minute information concerning all your dealings on eBay: items on which you're bidding; items you're selling; messages from eBay and others in the community; and all your preferences.

After you've opened your eBay account, this page will be fairly sparse. But, as soon as you become an active eBay community member, this page will burst to life. To help you get that process started, Chapter 4 discusses where to search for items to sell in your eBay auctions.

CHAPTER 4

# Inventory
# Resources

ONE OF THE MOST CLOSELY GUARDED SECRETS OF AN eBay PowerSeller is from where they source their items. It is hard to get a straight answer out of sellers on the topic, and that's just as it should be. Asking a PowerSeller for their product source secrets is like asking Aunt Berta for her secret cookie recipe—you can ask, but you risk being chased by an aggressive rolling pin.

The PowerSellers we spoke to told us that they continuously search for new sources of items. They search every step of the product life chain, from manufacturers to liquidators. And when they find a great source for items, they do all they can to protect and nurture that relationship. A good item source serves as the foundation for building a reliable and profitable business.

As every PowerSeller does, you will also need to do your own research of item sources. Below we've put together some great places to start your search, and a few qualities to look for in a good source.

## New Items

The source of your items depends largely on what you plan to sell. An eBay seller of new, high-end, computer memory and logic boards will have different sources than a seller of third-generation computer systems. So begin with a clear idea of what you plan to sell. If you plan to sell new items, make a list of the retailers and manufacturers that you know of within that product line. From that list you can begin to trace your way up and down the product's life chain to find the best place to buy. For example, if you are planning to sell new inkjet printers, the product life chain would look like this:

1. manufacturer (HP, Brother, Epson, etc.)
2. distributor (Vance Baldwin Electronics, Smart Surplus, Inc., Eastern Distributing, etc.)
3. wholesaler (CostCo, Ingram Micro, HorizonUSA, Over stockb2b.com, etc.)
4. retailer (CompUSA, BestBuy, Target, newegg.com, Tiger Direct, etc.)
5. liquidator (liquidation.com, txmicro.com, techliquidators.com, etc.)

Pick up the phone and call around to find the sale prices, policies, and restrictions at every step in the chain. Keep in mind that with every successive step in the chain away from the manufacturer, another middleman is added and the price goes up. So start with the manufacturer and work your way down.

## Manufacturers

More often than not, large manufacturers are set up (both physically and financially) to move products down the product life chain by the truckload, and are unwilling to take the time to sell in smaller quantities or deal with individual sales altogether. This makes buying directly from the manufacturer difficult. However, manufacturers also occasionally run into the problem of having too much inventory of a second- or third-generation item, which can take up valuable space in a warehouse. When on the phone with the manufacturer, be sure to ask if they have any overstocked, or "dead stock," items that you could help them liquidate. You'll be doing them a favor by clearing space for their first-generation equipment, and you'll be getting a good deal on older, but unused, equipment.

## Distributors

When speaking to an item's manufacturer, be sure to ask for their distributors. Call the distributors and ask them about becoming a reseller. They may require you to buy in large quantities or pay huge shipping costs, which may or may not work for your business model, but it could provide you with a great source if you can make it work. Be sure to crunch some numbers before you pick up the phone. Also, if you determine that you can, in fact, buy a truckload of 17-inch LCD monitors, be sure that you have the ability to store, sell, and track that amount of inventory. See more about inventory concerns in Chapter 12.

## *Wholesalers*

Wholesale clubs such as CostCo and Sam's Club should not be overlooked just because they are available to the general shopping public. They fall victim to the same problems of overstocking that plague many manufacturers. You may find deep discounts on desirable items sitting on the warehouse shelves just down the road from you. Just because an item isn't selling in your neck of the woods does not mean that there isn't high demand for it somewhere among the millions of eBay shoppers. Stick with trusted wholesalers, as most require a membership fee and some could turn out to be scammers.

## *Retailers*

Buying from retailers only makes sense when you can get a deal. Often sellers will find great deals from local retailers by buying up their customer returns. Some large retailers find it cheaper to destroy customer returns than it is to diagnose, fix, and restock them. So whether an item comes back to them because it is faulty, or just because it was an unwanted gift, the item is destroyed and the retailer absorbs the loss. By buying up customer returns, you get your items at a price significantly lower than retail, and the retailer recoups some loss. Just beware that customer-returned items are often faulty, and cannot be sold as new or reconditioned items without some repair. It may or may not be worth your time to test and repair items before reselling them.

Another option when sourcing from retailers is to buy their third-generation products. Many retailers provide an outlet for their third-generation goods as a way to clean off their shelves and recoup some losses from unsold merchandise. For example, CompUSA sells its unsold stock at auction over the web at www.compusawholesale.com. Ask the large retailers in your area if they have such a program.

## Liquidators

Many PowerSellers buy their items through liquidation, which is the last step in a new product's life chain. Items that are never sold to an end consumer are liquidated for a fraction of the retail price, often in bulk. You will find pallets of mostly old second- and third-generation items up for sale—

> We find a lot of equipment within our own company to sell, through our rentals and leasing channels. We also purchase products from computer wholesalers. We have found many at www.powersourceonline.com and through searches on the internet.
>
> —goodasnewcomputerscanada

sometimes all mixed in together. There are great deals to be had, for sure, but be careful when buying from liquidation companies. Most sell used goods from companies that are going out of business, or returned items from retail stores. If you're not careful about what you're buying, and from what company, you might end up stuck with a pallet load of damaged goods that are hard, or impossible to sell.

## Used Items

If you are planning on selling used items, you will need to follow a path different than those seeking new items. Your path will be a little less formal, a little more fun, and a little closer to home. The disadvantage to selling used items is that steady, reliable sources for quality items are hard to find. Steady sources of used items, such as the retail customer returns, as mentioned above, and liquidation services such as liquidation.com may provide you with a steady stream of items, though it will occasionally be polluted by faulty and unsaleable equipment.

In the following sections we've listed some great places to begin your search for items. Give each of these sources a chance, no matter how much you doubt their ability to produce results. One PowerSeller we spoke with stopped at a garage sale one morning that was only two miles from his home. He was ready to dismiss the whole affair as a lost cause, but came upon a several boxes full of second-generation networking routers and switches. While exciting in itself, the PowerSeller then learned that the home owner who was selling this equipment ran a company that sold first-generation networking equipment to large corporations across the country, and he not only had no use for this second-generation stuff, but also had an entire warehouse of it that he wanted to liquidate. The PowerSeller bought up all the networking equipment he could, from the garage sale and from the warehouse, and listed it on eBay. A few months later, his eBay business was booming and he was able to secure a deal for exclusive rights to buy all the future second-generation equipment that came into the warehouse. He found his largest supplier by visiting the back corner of a neighbor's garage.

## *Garage Sales*

Search for garage sales listed in your local classifieds, on bulletin boards, and along the roadsides in your area. Attend the sales in an order based on the likelihood that they will have computers for sale. Start with college communities, affluent suburbs, and established neighborhoods. New neighborhoods tend to have young families who are just starting out, and tend not to have too much of value to sell.

While searching in the papers for garage sales, keep an eye out for estate sales and moving sales as well. If you're in a college community, cruise around campus near the end of the spring semester. Many students sell off, or throw out, the contents of their dorm rooms to avoid packing it into the back of their Volvos. Sometimes you can pick up their printers, monitors, and bulky computers inexpensively.

## Local Auctions

Auctions, whether offered by a private organization or by the government, can be a great place to find computer equipment. Auction houses often sell off business equipment from bankruptcies, seized property from local police departments, and donated equipment from local closet cleaners. These auctions are often advertised in the local media, and occur fairly regularly. Call ahead to find out what type of items will be up for auction and, if the auction consists of a decent amount of equipment that you can sell in your store, it might be worth attending. Though be sure when bidding to keep your profit margin in mind. Don't let yourself get sucked into the bidding frenzy that makes auctions so successful. You could end up with the perfect item at a price too high to produce any profits for you.

## Newspaper Advertising

If after all the searching and running around you're getting tired of chasing inventory, why not let the merchandise come to you? You've probably seen ads in your local classifieds saying something akin to, "Cash For Computers!" or "We pay cash for your old PC!" They are there because they work. Place your phone number and e-mail address in the paper with a description of the type of equipment you're looking to buy, and people will start contacting you. This method will not provide you with all of your inventory, but, every so often, it will send a few computers or monitors or printers your way, saving you time and money. Once you've grown to a size large enough to handle sizable inventories, consider placing ads in larger classified markets and appropriate computer magazines.

## Buy Smart

Now that you've got a few good places to begin your hunt for computers and equipment to sell, you should begin to

> I get 90 percent of what I sell on eBay, actually. Other items I get are usually from my wife's school where they often try to raise money for the technology department through auctions.
>
> —chessmasterjack

think about how to buy smart. Going out and buying all the computers and accessories you can find will not produce a profitable business. It will fill your basement and empty your bank accounts. Before you begin buying, you must first find out what is selling, and at what price. Then, once you've got an idea of what will fly off the shelf and what will collect dust on it, you can take your knowledge and begin searching in the places listed above for the best-selling stuff, at the prices that will make you a profit.

The first place to begin is on eBay itself. Do a search of completed auctions, under the Advanced Search link on any page, for items similar to what you would like to sell. Take note of their final sale price, the number of bids they received, and the number of listings for this specific, or similar, items. Consider an item that received eight or more bids to be a hot item, meaning that there is significant demand for that item and the market could bear more like it for sale. If you find multiple completed listings for an item, each of which has eight or more bids, you've found an item worth selling. Your task then becomes to find that item, or the parts to build such an item, at a price that will produce profits when sold at the average sale price of the items in your search.

If you find an item that is heavily in demand and are able to list hundreds of that particular item, the average sales price will plummet, leaving you with little, if any, profits and a flooded market. Introduce your products slowly. There is a delicate balance of supply and demand, especially in the microcosm of an eBay category. Increase the number of your listings while keeping an eye fixed on the dropping average sale price of your products. Experiment with the balance between items sold per month and average sale price per item. You will find a point of maximum profitability.

If the item you're considering selling has many listings with less than eight, or zero, bids, you should either consider a different item, or a new approach to selling that item. The harsh reality is that not everything you want to sell will sell. If your dream is to build and sell hot pink computers, you're likely to be disappointed.

There are many free and commercial tools available to sellers to help them decide what to begin selling. eBay even has some of its own. See Chapter 10 for helpful product research tools.

CHAPTER 5

# Listing Items

FINALLY, IT IS TIME TO BEGIN SELLING. THIS CHAPTER WILL explain the best ways to get your computer equipment listed, seen, and sold. eBay is best known for its auctions, but provides other ways to sell as well. We'll begin with explaining how to list your items in an eBay auction, but we'll also explain eBay Stores and Fixed Price Listings—both of which provide great opportunities for sellers to move more computers.

## Auctions

To begin selling, click the Sell tab at the top of the main eBay page. You will be presented with a few options here, the number of which will depend on your feedback rating. Sellers with higher feedback ratings are presented with more selling options. First-timers are presented with Online Auction and Real Estate. Choose Online Auction, and continue.

## Categories

You will be presented with a large list of item categories from which to choose. For the purposes of selling computers, computer accessories, and computer equipment, the appropriate category for your auction is Computers & Networking.

Before continuing with Computers & Networking, take a moment to browse through the lengthy list of eBay top-level categories. You might come across a category that strikes your fancy, and could lead you to another business opportunity. That dusty box in the attic of Great-Grandma's scary stuffed bear collection could fetch a hefty paycheck in the lesser-known Dolls & Bears category.

Once you have clicked Computers & Networking, scroll down to select a second category for your auction if you wish. Choosing a second category for your auction will increase traffic to your listing, and ultimately it could raise your final sale price. However, don't be tempted to list your item in an inappropriate second category just for the sake of increasing traffic. Listing auctions in inappropriate categories violates the eBay User Agreement and comes with harsh penalties. In most cases, one category is sufficient.

## *Subcategories*

Now you must select a more specific sub-category of the top-level Computers & Networking category. The subcategory you choose will depend on the item you're selling. You will be presented with a number of interactive menus that will help you narrow down your category choice to a very specific sub-category. Choose, in every menu, the description that best fits your item. The menus will stop expanding once you have reached the most specific subcategory possible.

Choosing all these specifics helps eBay place your item into a category where it will be best found by buyers searching for your item. Choosing these subcategories carefully and correctly will improve your item's chances of being shown to the most interested buyers. Therefore, the item's chances of being sold, and of being sold at a good price, partly depend on your selections here.

For example, say that a fictional seller, Alex, built and wants to sell a PC. He would select Desktop PC in the first menu and then the processor size he used in the second menu. He installed a top-of-the-line Intel processor, and therefore selects "3.5GHZ, 3500+ & Higher" in the second menu, and "Intel Chip Sets" in the third. The fourth menu turns gray, and prompts Alex to continue below.

In another example, Jamie has chosen to buy and sell printers. He has just received a pallet of black and white, HP 8000 series, laser-jet printers and is in the process of listing some on eBay. eBay's expansive list of printers and their capabilities makes Jamie's job of listing easy. He simply chooses, in successive menus, "Printers —> Laser Printers —> HP —> Black & White —> 8000 Series."

Below the interactive menus, you will again be presented with the opportunity to choose a second top-level category. If you now wish to choose another category, click continue.

### Pre-Filling Information

For many items from major manufacturers, eBay will present you with an option to use their Pre-filled Information. This helpful feature will automatically fill in your item's auction listing with the manufacturer's default model information. In the example used above, Jamie's printers would be eligible for this option, and if he chose to use it, his auction listing for the printer would include the manufacturer's description of the printer, a stock photo of a new printer in that model, and model statistics such as model number, printing technology, output type, and print speed.

### Standard Listing

Alex's custom-built PC, obviously, would not be eligible for the Pre-filled Information option, and he would need to provide all the pertinent information about his PC manually. Most of the items you put up for auction will need to be listed in a similar way. Once you skip the Pre-filled Information option you will be presented with the page where you insert the item's title and description.

## Title and Description

The importance of writing effective titles and descriptions cannot be understated. Later in this book we will go into detail about what constitutes an effective title and description. But for the purpose of this logistics chapter, we'll give you a brief overview.

### *Item Title*

An auction title is limited to 55 characters. A character is defined as any letter, number, symbol, or space. The primary function of the title is to clearly state for bidders exactly what the item is that's up for auction. The secondary function of the title is to provide eBay's search program with the keywords it will use to display your auction in user searches. Balancing these two functions, while remaining under the 55-character limit, can be tricky. We'll provide you with some tips on how best to do this in Chapter 7.

### *Item Subtitle*

If you have a hard time fitting all the necessary information into your item's title, you can purchase the use of a subtitle for 50 cents. The item subtitle has the same limit of 55 characters as the item title, but the text in the subtitle is not included in eBay's search program. So be sure to fit all the critical search terms into the main title because any text you enter into the subtitle field will only serve to provide additional information to bidders.

PowerSellers sometimes use the subtitle to advertise additional non-critical information about the auction, such as low shipping charges, or to boast about their customer feedback score.

## *Item Specifics*

If your item was originally made by a major manufacturer such as Apple or Dell, chances are that eBay will provide you with an opportunity to detail your item's specifics. If you're listing a computer you'll be asked to specify the model, processor speed, amount of RAM, condition, and so on. If you're listing a printer, you'll be asked to specify if there are additional paper trays, extra RAM, and other added features. Specifying these details about your item will help eBay place it appropriately in search results, which only works to your advantage.

## *Item Description*

The auction description allows you more freedom than the title. There is no character limit, and the description box accepts plain text and HTML. Beginning users should use simple plain text format for the first few auctions, just to get the hang of setting up simple auctions. Plain text will look just like a simple text document. It will suffice as you're getting started, but you will want to become familiar with HTML so that you are able to take advantage of the immense formatting benefits it provides. For tips on how to use HTML in your listings, click on the HTML Tips link below the description text box.

We'll cover how to create effective and stunning description pages in Chapter 7. For now, you should write out the basic information regarding your item. Include the model number, the condition, the manufacturer, the configuration specifics, and anything else you can think to include. The more information you provide, the less time you'll spend answering e-mails from bidders.

## Pricing and Duration

On the next page you will be asked to provide the various prices, auction duration, and photos for your item's listing. There are strategies to each of these pieces of your auction, a few of which we will cover in Chapter 6. In this chapter, we will focus on defining the terminology used on this page.

### Starting Price

The auction's starting price is the amount you set to be the minimum opening bid. If your item sells, it will sell for at least the amount you enter here. The safest strategy is to enter the lowest amount you would be willing to accept for the item.

### Reserve Price

Setting a reserve price is optional. If set, the amount entered here will act as a safety net for sellers. If bidding does not reach the amount you set for the reserve price, you are not obligated to sell your item. When a reserve price is set, bidders are notified of that fact on the auction's page, though the amount of the reserve price is hidden to encourage bidding.

### *Buy It Now Price*

The Buy It Now price, or BIN, is a price you can offer to buyers who might want to forego the bidding process and purchase the item immediately. Once a bidder chooses to pay your BIN price, the auction ends. Setting a BIN price is a good idea as it opens up your item to a new market of convenience buyers who do not like to participate in bidding, and are happy to pay a higher price to receive the item more quickly.

### *Donate Percentage of Sale*

eBay's Giving Works program allows you to dictate whether or not you would like to donate a portion of the item's ultimate sale price to charity, and, if so, what percentage. If you choose to donate some of your proceeds to charity, eBay will present you with hundreds of nonprofit organizations from which to choose. After selecting an organization from the list, and selecting the percentage of the sale price you would like to donate, eBay will handle the rest.

### *Duration*

Seven days is the standard length of an eBay auction. You are able to choose from one-, three-, five-, and seven-day listings for the standard listing fee. If you would like your auction to run for ten days, eBay will charge you an extra 40 cents. Most PowerSellers use the standard seven-day auction. Auctions are easier to keep track of when you can plan on an auction ending exactly one week from when you submitted it.

## Fixed Price Listings

Technically, a fixed price listing is not an auction because there is no bidding, but those listings show up in auction search results. This format allows users to buy and sell items immediately at a set price, with no bidding or waiting. You can sell more than one of an item in a fixed price listing, which saves you time and money in listing fees.

## Private Listing

Private listings are available for sellers who require anonymity for their bidders during an auction. During a private auction, bidders' user IDs are not displayed on the auction's page or in the bidding history. Only the seller can view the IDs of the different bidders. Setting up a private auction may be appropriate for high-priced items, or items that are so in demand that a buyer would benefit from remaining anonymous. Computer sellers are not likely to require private listings.

## Start Time

The day and time that your auction ends depends on when your auction begins and the duration you have set. There are two ways to dictate when your auction will end. First, you can submit your auction at the specific time of day that you would like the auction to end, and, when the duration you have set expires, it will end accordingly. Or, for an additional 10 cents, eBay allows you to schedule the time your auction will start, thereby freeing you to submit your auction whenever you have time.

Most bidding on any particular auction occurs within the last few minutes. This is because as an auction nears its end, it moves up in eBay's auction list when it is sorted in the default "Time: ending soonest" order. Also, savvy bidders have learned not to place bids early to prevent other bidders from outbidding them. Rather, they wait until the final few seconds of an auction to place their maximum bid. This way, they keep the final sale price low and improve their chances of sneaking in the last bid. This practice is called "sniping."

Due to sniping, PowerSellers make a point of ending their auctions during eBay's peak traffic times. Auctions that end during peak hours receive substantially more bids due to the higher number of bidders on the site to see their auction when it is at the top of the list. As a general rule, Sunday evenings, between 6 P.M. and midnight (EST) tend to be eBay's highest traffic times. There are exceptions, of course, such as Super Bowl Sunday when eBay traffic, and internet traffic as a whole, plummets.

## Quantity

eBay allows sellers to post auctions that have one or more items for sale. If you are selling one item only, you will not need to specify a quantity. If you are selling multiple items, there are several ways to do so.

**INDIVIDUAL ITEMS.** If you wish to sell more than one of an identical item, eBay allows you to specify a quantity for an auction provided you meet the following requirements. You must be:

- ID verified
- or have a feedback rating of 30 or more and have been registered on eBay for more than 14 days
- or have a PayPal account, accept PayPal payments, and have a feedback score of 15 or higher

Multiple item auctions work differently than single item auctions. Bidders submit their offered price and the number of items they wish to purchase. The winning bid has the highest total price, which equals the offered price multiplied by the number of items requested. All winning bidders pay the lowest successful offered price.

**LOTS.** If you would like to sell many items in one bunch instead of piecing them out separately, you can sell them as a single lot. You will need to specify the number of identical items that are in the lot and provide a description of the items.

Bidders will bid on the lot as a whole instead of for one individual item. The winning bidder takes them all.

## Item Location

This address should be set to the location from which you do your shipping. It is used by buyers to calculate accurate shipping costs, which many bidders smartly factor into their bids.

## Add Pictures

Pictures are a critical piece of your auction. Auctions without photos sell poorly, or not at all. Bidders like to see the items on which they're bidding. eBay provides two methods for placing photos in your auctions. Sellers can use eBay's own Basic Picture Services, or a third-party web host.

eBay Basic Picture Services. If you choose to use eBay's picture services, your first photo is included in the listing price. Every additional photo you choose to insert costs 15 cents. To upload photos using this service, simply click the "Browse" button and locate the appropriate photos on your computer.

Your Web Hosting. To include a photo for free from a third-party web host, you must first upload the photo to your web server, and then enter the address to that photo into the text field here. The address should look something like this:

www.yourwebhost.com/ebay/photos/item1.jpg. If everything is correct, the image will be displayed in your auction.

## Listing Designer

To help you spice up your auction description, eBay offers the Listing Designer. For an additional 10 cents, this tool allows you to add colorful borders to your listing and select an attractive photo layout. There are quite a few templates from which to choose, so choose carefully and try to find one that is appropriate for the item being auctioned.

## Increase your Item's Visibility

eBay provides plenty of options that allow you to set your listing apart from the others. Some are worth the additional cost, some are not.

**GALLERY.** This option will display a thumbnail image of your item in search results and listings. Studies show that using this feature increases final sale price by as much as 11 percent. It is well worth the 35 cent price.

**SUBTITLE.** A subtitle provides a good opportunity to present more information about your item to bidders in search results and category listings. It has not been shown to increase sale price or conversion rate, so judge for yourself whether or not the extra information this would allow you to display is worth the 50 cents.

**Bold.** Selecting the bold option will bold your auction's title in search results and listings. Bolding has been shown to improve final sale price by 7 percent. It costs $1.

**Border.** Adding a border to your listing is a great way to separate it from other auctions. If this option is selected, a colorful thin border will be placed around your auction listing in search results and category lists. Expect this option to boost final sale price also by about 7 percent. A border costs $3, and therefore is only worth the expense on high-priced or important promotional auctions.

**Highlight.** At $5 this is the most expensive aesthetic upgrade you can purchase for your listing. Adding a highlight will fill in a colorful background behind your auction listing in search results and category lists. When coupled with a gallery photo, this option really makes your listing stand out. Generally, it increases final sale price by as much as 15 percent.

### *Promote Your Listing on eBay*

For high-priced or important promotional auctions, eBay offers sellers the chance to advertise their auctions in different "featured" locations across the site. These options are expensive, so they are best used sparingly to attract bidders into auctions that will either fetch a high price, or will funnel bidders via cross-promotion into your eBay store and other auctions.

**FEATURED PLUS!** At the top of search result pages, eBay displays featured auctions above the regular search results. For $19.95 you can place your auction in the featured spot above appropriate search results listings. This option, while expensive, increases the final sale price of your item by a whopping 76 percent. This option also does a great job of funneling bidders into your auction, and into your eBay store.

**GALLERY FEATURED.** This option is similar to the Featured Plus! option above. However, instead of featuring your auction title at the top of all search result and listing pages, this option will display a thumbnail image of your item's first image along with your auction title at the top of the results page when seen in Gallery view. This option is $19.95 and because it is new to eBay, there is no statistical performance information available yet.

**HOME PAGE FEATURED.** This option is eBay's biggest promotional opportunity. It is quite expensive at $39.95 for one item, and $79.95 for two or more items, but it provides the chance for your auction to appear on eBay's main home page—one of the internet's most popular sites. This option increases bidding on your item by 58 percent. Again, this is a great promotional tool when used correctly.

## Gift Services

If you would like to suggest that your item would make a nice gift for someone, you can select to place a gift icon next to your listing title for 25 cents. If you choose to advertise your item as a gift, you have the option of advertising the following services: gift wrapping, express shipping, and shipping to a gift recipient instead of the buyer.

### Page Counter

A page counter is a basic tool that allows you to see the number of times your auction has been visited. There is no charge to include a counter on your auction page.

## Payment Methods

As we mentioned earlier, there are several methods for collecting payment from auction winners. If you have registered for a PayPal account, and indicated in your eBay preferences that you would like to accept PayPal payments from buyers, your PayPal information will appear here. If you have chosen to avoid PayPal, you have several options: Money Order/Cashier's Check, Personal Check, and Other/See Item Description. If you select Other/See Item Description you will need to be sure that you state your "Other" payment terms in your

> I don't run into fraud often, but I do about every six months. I've lost money due to it, sometimes because I have not done my research properly; sometimes because I've taken chances that I knew at the time I probably shouldn't.
> 
> —chessmasterjack

auction's description. If you have your own merchant account, you can select that you accept Visa/MasterCard, Discover, or American Express through your own terminal.

## Ship-To Locations

There are two main options when specifying your shipping terms: Will ship, and will not ship. If you are interested in only selling to local buyers, and do not require shipping, then you should choose "Will not ship." For all other sellers, you must choose "Will ship . . ." and then select the countries to which you're willing to send items.

> We run into fraud attempts every day. We quickly learned how to detect fraud and we have pretty well eliminated all fraudulent orders. We simply cancel fraudulent orders before they are shipped.
>
> —goodasnewcomputerscanada

Shipping internationally can be risky as much of the fraud that occurs on eBay is perpetrated by people outside the United States—particularly the famous "Nigeria" scam. Some PowerSellers refuse to ship any items outside the United States to reduce risk of falling victim to scams. Other Power Sellers have no qualms with shipping worldwide. Decide for yourself which best suits you and your business. Though, if you do decide to ship internationally, be cautious. Take extra precaution to make sure that your payment clears, that the address is legitimate, and that all the proper customs forms are filled out accurately.

## Shipping and Sales Tax

There are three main options when setting your shipping preferences: flat fee, calculated fees, and freight.

### Flat

If you would like to designate a flat shipping rate for all your items to all locations, you can do so in the first shipping tab. You can select up to three different carriers and specify the fees you will charge for each.

### Calculated

To more closely estimate what the shipping charges will be for individual bidders, you can choose to use a calculated rate. To do so, you must enter the item's shipping weight and dimensions, and then select up to three carriers. Upon winning an auction the buyer will insert his or her zip code and the fees will be calculated accordingly. If you are looking to make shipping and handling a profit source, this method will not work for you.

### Freight

For large items over 150 pounds, eBay offers freight shipping options. For sellers of computers and computer accessories, freight shipping will most likely not be necessary—unless you're selling 1970s mainframes. If you find that you need freight shipping, simply follow the steps on the freight tab and your auction will be marked accordingly.

## Sales Tax

If your state requires you to charge sales tax on internet purchases, you will need to select your state from the pull-down menu and enter the tax rate in the text field. If your state does not require you to charge tax, leave this blank.

## Return Policy

If you are planning on accepting returns on items, you will need to check the Returns Accepted box and then fill in the terms under which you will accept returns.

## Payment Instructions

If you require special payment instructions, use this field to state them for your bidders. Even if you do not require special payment arrangements, it is a good idea to reiterate your Payment Policies here. You can never be too clear when dealing with your buyers.

## Review and Submit

Now that you have configured your auction as you would like, eBay gives you the opportunity to review all the decisions you've made and edit anything that needs fixing. Double check every piece of your auction for accuracy. Spell check your title, description, and shipping and payment policies. It is important that you present everything professionally.

Your auction listing fees will be displayed at the bottom of this page. If everything looks in order, click "submit" and begin your auction. If you have not chosen to schedule your auction, it will begin immediately and end after the duration you've chosen expires.

Congratulations, you've submitted your first auction on eBay! Now you get to sit back and watch the bidders bid. Good luck!

## eBay Stores

Along with putting merchandise up for auction on eBay, you may want to consider opening an eBay Store, which would allow you to sell your fixed price and auction items from a unique destination on eBay. eBay Stores make it easy to cross-sell your inventory and build repeat business.

According to eBay, you should open an eBay Store if you want all your listings displayed in one customizable place; if you want to be able to easily generate repeat business and encourage multiple purchases from the same buyers; if you want to control what you cross-sell to your customers; and if you want to maintain a larger permanent inventory than you can selling through auctions.

eBay Stores offer a convenient selling platform for all your eBay listings—auctions, fixed price items, and store inventory. eBay promotes stores in several ways. All your auction listings will contain the eBay Store icon; when bidders click on that icon, they are taken to your store. That icon is also attached to your eBay User ID for increased visibility. The eBay Store directory is designed to promote all stores and will drive buyers to your particular store. You will also receive your own personalized eBay Store web site address that you can distribute and publicize as you wish.

The process of opening an eBay Store is almost as simple as setting up your initial User ID. The only requirements are that you be a registered eBay seller and have a minimum feedback rating of 20 or be ID-verified.

Any items that you have in active listings at the time you open your store will not appear in your store. But any auctions or fixed priced listing you post once your store is opened will automatically appear in your eBay Store.

The cost of a basic eBay Store is a nominal monthly fee (current rates can be found at www.ebay.com) that increases with the level of services you desire, along with additional fees for items listed and sold. Store inventory listings are less expensive than auction listings and appear for a longer time. However, those listings appear only in your store and do not come up in traditional eBay auction searches. In addition to insertion fees, as with auctions, you also pay final-value fees when an item in a store listing sells.

eBay offers three store levels: basic, featured, and anchor. All have their own customizable storefront and the ability to list store inventory, but featured and anchor stores include additional services. Here's how the three levels differ from one another:

1. *Basic.* Your store is automatically listed in the eBay Stores Directory and will appear in every category directory where you have items listed.

2. *Featured.* Your store rotates through a special featured section on the eBay Stores home page; receives priority placement in "related stores" on search and listings pages; and it is featured within the category directory pages where you have items listed. In addition, you receive monthly reports on your sales and marketplace performance.
3. *Anchor.* In addition to the services offered to featured stores, your store can be showcased with your logo within the eBay Stores directory pages. It will also receive premium placement in "related stores" on search and listings pages, which means your store will be placed higher on the page than the featured stores.

Check the eBay web site for current store subscription fees.

## *Setting Up Your Store*

You want to apply the same principles to stocking your eBay Store as you would a bricks-and-mortar store. eBay allows you to create up to 300 custom categories for your products, similar to aisles in a physical store.

You may decide to use product-based categories or you might use a more flexible system, with categories like "sale items," "bestsellers," and "seasonal." Consider having a category for new items so people who visit your store regularly can quickly see what you've added recently. These custom categories can be changed and updated as often as you wish, which is a significant benefit to a seller whose inventory changes frequently.

> **TIP**
>
> Be sure to use your store to list all the items you have in your inventory that complement your active auctions, and be sure to mention your store in all your eBay listings.

Your store site should also clearly explain how you operate. Take advantage of the Store Policies page to provide a complete and professional description of your policies and procedures. Use About My Store to establish your credentials and provide some history about you and your company. Make sure that each store listing incorporates the same features as a traditional auction with a good title, clear pictures, and adequate description.

## Use Your Store to Cross-Sell and Up-Sell

All eBay Store subscriptions have the advantage of strategically placing promotion boxes in storefronts on different pages that can highlight featured items, provide special announcements, or be used in a variety of ways to showcase your store.

You also get cross-promotion tools that help you up-sell by allowing you to control which items your buyers see after they bid on or buy one of your items, or use the checkout function after a transaction has ended. You can choose different items to show on each listing.

The tools work by allowing you to establish "merchandising relationships" for the items you list; this determines which items the buyers will be shown. You determine what goes together by designating relationships for as many or as few items as you'd like. If you don't include cross-merchandise on one of your items, eBay will automatically select related items you are selling to display to your buyers.

### *Understand the Commitment*

Your eBay Store is open for business 24/7, whether you're awake or asleep. You need to monitor your store closely, answer questions from shoppers promptly, ship merchandise on schedule and as promised, and deal with any other customer service issues that might arise as soon as possible.

If you go on vacation or are going to be away from your store for any reason, you can either arrange for someone else to monitor the site and take care of your business or you can place your store "on vacation" with eBay for an indefinite period. This will essentially place your store on "pause" until you return. However, you will continue to be charged the normal store subscription and listing fees.

CHAPTER 6

# Pricing

*P*RICING IS A CONTENTIOUS ISSUE AMONG EBAY PowerSellers. Some swear by setting a low Starting Price and a high Reserve Price, whereas others avoid Reserve Prices outright fearing that they sabotage the auction's final sale price and result in lower profits per item. There is no right answer, and the method that will work best for you depends largely on the nature of your target bidders, the popularity of your auctions, and the retail price of your items.

This chapter will provide you with an introduction to all the different prices you'll need to set when creating an auction, and the strategies used by PowerSellers when setting those prices. You will need to tinker with these different strategies to find the ones that produce the highest profits for you.

## Starting Price

An auction's Starting Price is the lowest amount that the first bidder will need to bid to participate in the auction. Many sellers make the case that this Starting Price should be set to the lowest amount that you're willing to accept for an item while retaining an acceptable profit margin. If your aim is to make a 20 percent profit on everything you sell, then this price should simply be set to 20 percent higher than what it cost you to buy, pack, and ship the item. This method is most near traditional brick-and-mortar pricing methods because it guarantees profitability. But, like traditional brick-and-mortar pricing methods, it does not guarantee sales.

The next pricing methods are more suited to eBay's dynamic and fluid pricing phenomena. Sellers who are willing to gamble their profit margin are more likely to create the eBay buyer bidding frenzy. The aim of this strategy is to create a frenzy around every auction by capitalizing on a bidder's competitive drive to win. This frenzy, when created successfully, drives up the item's final sale price and awards higher profits to the seller. How does one create this frenzy? There are a few ways to do it.

### One Dollar, Low Reserve

First is the "$1LR" method, or the "One Dollar, Low Reserve" method. This strategy begins by setting a $1, or lower, starting price on an item. The item could be either an old keyboard worth ten bucks, or a high-end computer system worth $4,000—the item's real-world value is not taken into account. The low starting price encourages bargain-hunting bidders to jump into the auction early. The increased number of bidders sends your item's price skyward during the auction, whittling out the less enthusiastic bidders as the price goes up. But many of the original bidders will remain, either because they know the $1LR tactic and have expected to pay a fair price for the item from the beginning, or because they are now emotionally invested in the auction and feel compelled to win. Each bid, whether by calculation or compulsion, drives up your item's price.

Listing expensive inventory for $1 would frighten any reasonable businessperson. Therefore, this method includes a safety net in the Low Reserve price set at the auction's outset. This reserve price should be set low enough that bidders do not become discouraged when their bids repeatedly do not surpass the hidden reserve price, yet high enough that you don't lose your profits when the item sells. One of the keys to making this strategy work is that you must advertise that you have set a Low Reserve somewhere in your auction. Every bidder will see that you have set a reserve price, but the amount of that reserve is hidden from them. Reserve prices tend to scare off bidders who are skeptical that sellers are overvaluing their items, and making the reserve prices too near retail prices. Therefore, for this strategy to work, you must set the price low, and advertise that you have done so.

## One Dollar, No Reserve

The most controversial pricing method is known as the "$1NR" method, or, as you may have guessed, the "One Dollar, No Reserve" method. This strategy is similar to the above strategy, though it is far riskier in that without setting a reserve price, your blazingly fast 3 GHz Pentium 4 gaming machine might very well sell for a dollar, leaving you with the huge financial loss. Many sellers use this strategy successfully, trusting that if they have promoted the item well enough, the eBay bidding community will determine the fair market value for the item. And, because the hope of buying a high-end machine for only a few dollars draws in a large number of early bidders, there is a greater chance of a bidding war developing and driving profits through the roof.

Be cautious when using or experimenting with the $1NR strategy. It often falls victim to sniping, wherein savvy bidders wait until the closing seconds of an auction to place a bid, thereby not allowing time for the item's price to reach fair market value and securing a huge bargain. This method also should not be used alone, as it can prevent the growth of a business by limiting the number of similar items that can be sold at one time—the higher number of items available will lower the demand for that item, and therefore your final selling price. The $1NR method is best used as a promotional tool to draw bidders into auctions, where the seller is cross-promoting their auctions that use not-so-risky pricing strategies.

It should be noted that if you choose to use either the $1LR or $1NR method of pricing, setting your Starting Price at 99 cents instead of one dollar would work just as effectively in drawing in bidders, but would also save you money in listing fees due to eBay's listing fee structure.

## *Buy It Now (BIN)*

The BIN price caters to convenience buyers who would rather pay your asking price than wait a week for your auction to end. Over 25 percent of the items sold on eBay are sold through stores, BIN, or other fixed price sales. So, to choose not to set a BIN price is to choose not to sell to a substantial number of your buyers. It should be used as an important part of your overall pricing strategy.

The first BIN method applies if you have opted for a conservative pricing strategy and set your Starting Prices at a level that would produce a profit. By setting your BIN price slightly higher than your Starting Price, you can encourage bidders to bypass the lengthy bidding process and purchase the item immediately. It may be worth the few extra dollars to them to skip the days of watching and bidding. This method works well with relatively inexpensive items that are not likely to create a bidding frenzy, or with items that are in high demand, where you are confident that you will receive your asking price.

The second BIN method is used in conjunction with the $1NR promotional strategy. By setting a BIN price within a

> We sell items mostly through Buy It Now. We find that premium used products do not get bid up high enough to cover our costs. We do many auctions for all our grade "B" products. For example, any item that has a flaw, such as a laptop with a scratched screen, is auctioned. We try to have auctions and Buy It Now items closing every day.
>
> —goodasnewcomputers

$1NR auction, you are achieving two things: attracting a high number of potential convenience buyers, and planting a suggestion in the minds of the bidders as to what is a fair price for the item at auction. eBay buyers are smart and often do research, both on eBay and off, to find the fair market value for the item you are selling. But that doesn't mean that setting a BIN price for them to bid toward will not affect bidding habits.

## Reserve Price

There is little strategy behind setting a Reserve Price. Bidders tend to opt for auctions without a set Reserve Price due to the promise of a better bargain, and therefore they should be used sparingly. Though, if you are testing a new item to see what kind of bids it produces, or cannot bear to see it sell for less than a certain amount, then a Reserve Price is a good idea. PowerSellers rarely use Reserves, and in some cases, when they do opt to use a Reserve Price, they go so far as to state what the reserve price is in the item's description. This provides the seller with a price guarantee, and the bidder with the knowledge of how much they would need to pony up. This method is unconventional and rarely used as setting your Starting Price would produce the same effective result, but it is worth consideration.

## *Profitability versus Risk*

Finding an effective pricing strategy is an exercise in balancing profitability and risk. A high-risk strategy may yield a few highly profitable sales, but it will not do so reliably. A conservative strategy can ensure that every sale you make is reliably profitable, but sales could be slow or yield small profits.

The most effective pricing plan makes use of a combination of these strategies. High-risk strategies are effective in attracting the attention of bidders. Use cross-promotion within those high-risk auctions as promotional tools for your low-risk auctions, fixed price items, and store. Soon, your high-risk auctions will be leading bidders into your other, more reliably profitable, sales channels within eBay.

> We very rarely do No Reserve auctions. I am sure they have their place, but they do not fit with my business goals. I don't see them as being harmful. Once in a while a buyer gets lucky and wins something for well below market value. But, that is one of the great lures of eBay!
>
> —somersetsales

CHAPTER 7

# Selling
# Your Items

Now that you're familiar with the logistics of starting an auction on eBay, it is time for some fine tuning. To receive the highest price for your items you will need to put some thought and care into your item's auction. There are three main areas: the title, the description, and the photos.

The importance of creating quality titles, descriptions, and photos in your auctions cannot be understated. This is your opportunity to communicate directly to buyers. With the competition as fierce as it is in the Computers & Networking category, you must communicate effectively.

## The Title

The auction title has two important jobs. First, it provides the keywords that eBay uses to produce results when buyers use the site's search function. Most buyers find their items through eBay's search function, and although it is possible for buyers to search both title and description, the site's default setting searches only auction titles. So be sure when writing your title that you use any keywords that a buyer might use when searching for your item. Remember, the title has a limit of 55 characters.

Second, the title should provide potential bidders with as much information as possible about the auction while remaining readable. Here are some things to keep in mind when writing your titles. Always include, if available:

- Manufacturer's name
- Model number
- Item condition
- Pertinent configuration information (memory, CPU speed, HD capacity, etc.)

Be sure to avoid:

- Space-wasting attention grabbers (L@@K!!)
- ALL CAPS
- Unconventional abbreviations
- Adjectives (Use these in your description.)

Here are two auction titles for the same computer.

*Good Title*
P4 3.2GHz 1GB DDR2, DVDRW 160GB SATA GeForce Computer

*Bad Title*
AWESOME!!! Custom Gamer PC with FAST Processor/ RAM GR8!

The first title is packed with information to help the buyer know exactly what is up for auction. It contains keywords that a buyer would use to search for such a computer, and all of the abbreviations used are industry standards that buyers seeking this high-end computer would know. The second title may catch the bidder's eye more readily among the other titles on the page, but it contains few keywords and wastes space with exclamation points, useless adjectives, and spelling out words that can be abbreviated. Not only would this second title not come up in searches, it gives the bidder no useful indication of what they will see if they look at this auction. The bidder will not waste time with this listing and move on.

## Description

Investing time in writing a good description will pay off in the price you receive. Your description should include:
- the name of the item;
- what the item is made of;

- when and where it was made;
- who made it (company, artist, designer, author, etc.);
- what condition its in;
- weight, size, and/or dimensions;
- notable features or markings;
- and any special background or history.

Everything in your description should be true and accurate. If an item is damaged or missing parts, do not say something vague, such as "easily restored." If possible, identify exactly what needs to be replaced or suggest the buyer purchase the item to be used as parts for another piece. You might also add a personal touch to your description; many sellers have found that doing so can increase bids and sales. For example, specifically say what you like about the item, whom it would appeal to and why, or how it could be used. If the item is not in perfect condition, be honest. Describe any scratches, chips, stains, and other imperfections.

Avoid something known as keyword spamming—including words in your description that are not actually related to your item just because they are words a search would pick up. This is against eBay's listing policies. However, do use as many legitimate search words and phrases in your description as possible to be sure your item will come up when bidders search.

You can also use your description to add details about shipping costs, payment terms, and any other details you think may be of interest to a bidder.

Even if you plan to charge a precise shipping cost, it's always a good idea to include at least an estimate of the shipping costs so bidders aren't surprised when the auction is over. Also, let bidders know if there are any restrictions on where you will ship, such as United States only, United States and Canada only, or to certain international locations. eBay has a shipping calculator that you can insert in your auctions that allows the buyer to determine how much it will cost to send that specific item to their address via the United States Postal Service (USPS) or UPS. When you're finished, proofread, spell check, and proofread again.

## Make Your Pictures Worth More Than 1,000 Words

A photo, indicated by a camera icon or a thumbnail image of your item in an auction list, will make a tremendous difference in the success of your auctions. Quality photos not only let bidders see what your product really looks like, but they also say that you're a serious, professional eBay seller.

Create a photo area in your home or shop with good lighting and a backdrop for an uncluttered background. Consider developing a photo backdrop with a distinctive color, pattern, logo, or company name that helps brand your business. If appropriate, showcase your item with accessories to display it to its best advantage. Be sure to indicate whether or not those accessories are included in the auction, are available separately, or are not for sale. A box draped with a piece of plain fabric

> We take pictures, edit them to our satisfaction, and then post them to our web site. We have a standard background that we use. And our two-megapixel camera is fine for the pictures we take for eBay.
>
> —notebooksauction-dot-com

works as a display pedestal. Maintain a database of pictures so its easy to pull up images for listings when you are selling items you've sold before.

Invest in a digital camera. You don't have to get the top-of-the-line model, but get a camera that has more than two megapixels and a macro function for clear close-up shots. Your customers will want to see the insides of computers, the scratches on any printers, dead pixels on any monitors, and so on. Therefore, a macro function for clarity up close is important.

If you have a scanner, you can use print film and then scan your photos. However, this process is time consuming and costly. If you plan to sell on eBay with any regularity, invest in a digital camera.

Once you have the pictures uploaded to your computer you can then use an image editing program to adjust and enhance your images. Be sure that all the parts of the image are bright and clear.

## *Copyrights*

When writing your descriptions and uploading your photos, be sure that you are using original content. The practice of cutting and pasting item descriptions from a manufacturer's web site is common because it makes quick work of providing accurate information. However, this practice can be dangerous as some manufacturers copyright the promotional materials for their products. If you choose to use text or photos from an outside source in your auction listings, be sure that it is not copyrighted material. If you see no copyright symbol, don't assume that it is free to use. Contact the company and ask for permission to use their photos or text. Most manufacturers are happy to give you permission. Though it only takes one disgruntled corporate lawyer to ruin your day. When in doubt, it is best to create original content.

CHAPTER 8

# Customer Care

*E*VEN BEFORE YOU SUBMIT YOUR AUCTION TO EBAY, YOU must be thinking about customer care. eBay bidders are sophisticated people, and care every bit as much about the way they are treated as the real-world retail shopper. This proper treatment begins when you are putting together your item's auction page.

## Pre-Auction

Bidders expect your auction page to be professional, attractive, error-free, and easy to use. If your page has typos, incorrect information, fuzzy photos, or simply hard-to-read bricks of text, bidders will shop somewhere else. Take extra care to consider your bidders when formatting and writing your auction pages. Be sure to invite bidders to contact you with questions. In addition to eBay's "Ask seller a question" link, provide an e-mail address and phone number where you can be reached with questions. Make it as easy as possible for bidders to do business with you.

When writing your descriptions, try to anticipate questions bidders might ask you. Answer any hypothetical questions you can think of. Taking some extra time when writing your descriptions will save you loads of time in answering e-mails and phone calls.

## During Auctions

During auctions you will need to be available to your customers in case a few of them need to ask you a question. As any PowerSeller will tell you, answering questions from bidders will quickly become a lot of work.

### Skype

In 2005, eBay purchased the online VoIP (Voice-Over-Internet-Protocol) company Skype. Skype offers a free, downloadable program that installs on all major operating systems. The company has over 113 millions registered users in over 225 countries around the globe. Their program enables users to make free voice "telephone" calls from their computer to anyone in the world who is also running Skype. Or, for a low per minute rate, Skype users can also send and receive calls to and from regular telephone lines.

This is a good move for eBay as communication is at the heart of every successful eBay sale. eBay exists because of its ability to bring together buyers and sellers from all over the world. By integrating Skype into its services, eBay will provide sellers with the ability to offer free voice communication during a sale no matter if the buyer is in Boston or Boca Raton. For more information visit www.skype.com.

## *Questions*

Answering questions from bidders can become a tiresome and frustrating task. There will be nights when you are tired, it is 2 A.M., and you've got 50 more questions to answer. It is during these times that you must keep your feedback score in mind. Be polite and professional in your answers. If you are receiving the same question over and over again, write a polite and thorough answer once and then cut and paste it to the 20 people who need it. If the question comes to you through the eBay message center, it will be posted on the auction's page for future questioners to see. The more patient you are with your customers, the more loyal they will be to you in the future.

There will come a point when you will need to hire someone to help you slog through all the questions. When selling technical items, such as computers, you will receive more questions than most sellers. People understand how a shirt works or a book, but, for example, they may need your help figuring out whether the motherboard you're selling will

> In our opinion, it's not a good idea to automate too much of a mail order business. Simple online shopping carts linked to easy payment options is helpful, but you need to keep your phone, fax, and e-mail open to buyers. Dealers and business clients want to talk to a real person before ordering for the first time.
>
> —mcpricebreakers

work with the processor they just bought. Make sure when you hire someone to help you answer questions, that he or she is as knowledgeable about your products are you are.

## Post-Auction

Once an auction ends, be sure to contact the winner right away to congratulate him or her and present the next steps. Constant and clear communication will help the transaction occur smoothly. As soon after the end of the auction as you can, send an invoice with the item number, the auction's total price, and instructions for submitting payment to you. Be sure to thank the winner for his or her business and to give the e-mail a personal tone. For a nominal fee, eBay will automate this for you. Many PowerSellers take advantage of this option, but caution new sellers to make sure that the e-mail does not sound automated. Customers would rather deal with a person than a machine, even though sometimes it just isn't feasible for sellers.

After the winning bidder has submitted payment, they will expect a receipt and quick shipment of their item. Many PowerSellers, when they do receive negative feedback, receive it because the bidder was disappointed with the speed of shipping. If you cannot ship an item immediately for some reason, be sure that you contact the buyer and make them aware of the delay. If you know about a possible delay prior to posting an auction, mention it in the auction's description. It is better to be honest than disappointing.

Once the payment has been received and the package has been shipped, e-mail the bidder to let him know that his item is on the way. If you have shipped via a carrier that uses a tracking number, include that in the e-mail so that the bidder can watch expectantly as it approaches his house.

Then, once the transaction is complete, provide timely positive feedback if warranted. If you've done everything right, you will be rewarded with positive feedback in return. Remember, you cannot make everyone happy, although as evidenced by the overwhelmingly positive feedback ratings of some PowerSellers, it is possible to come pretty darn close.

## When Things Go Wrong

Sometimes you will make mistakes. For the most part, buyers are understanding people and will be forgiving if you are straightforward with them. When mistakes happen, do what you need to do to make things right for the customer.

> Very rarely do we have any fraud issues. We do get emails from someone overseas that wants to pay via COD, or the common "Nigeria" scam. eBay has done a wonderful job on attacking and reducing the latter.
>
> —somersetsales

> We run into fraud three to five times daily. Be careful.
> 
> —notebooksauction-dot-com

Remember, this is your business; you have the power and authority to do what needs to be done. Don't hesitate to offer a partial or full refund if it means keeping a customer.

If you run into a belligerent customer who cannot be reasoned with, remain calm. You may receive unpleasant e-mails or worse from angry customers, but you must not allow it to affect how you deal with the problem. Read the customer's entire e-mail, apologize for the problem, ask him or her how you can best solve the dilemma, and then thank him or her for their patience and understanding . . . even if they showed you none. You will be surprised how many irate customers can be turned into grateful customers with a polite and apologetic e-mail.

## Beware of Scams

One of the most well-known scams on eBay occurs when a winning bidder receives an item from the seller and immediately contacts the seller with a complaint of some sort. Most times the buyer will complain of damage during shipping, or misstated condition of the item, or an incorrect shipment. The buyer will then demand a full or partial refund and threaten to post negative feedback to the seller if he or she does not comply. As as seller, it would seem that you have two poor options: comply or take the negative feedback. But that is not the case. If you deem the item worth the cost of attempting recovery, you have a third option. In your best pleasant and understanding tone, apologize for the damage/mistake and offer either an exchange if you have an identical item in stock, or a full refund upon receipt of the damaged or incorrect item. In this scenario you may need to cough up the return shipping charges, but at least you're not losing the value of the item or being scammed out of honestly earned revenue.

## Conflict Resolution

eBay will rarely provide aid in a conflict between a buyer and seller. You are pretty much on your own to settle conflicts professionally. However, eBay will come to your aid in certain circumstances. Here are a few:

- ebay receives a court order finding that feedback you've received is slanderous or illegal in some way.

> Feedback can make or break you. Get it as high as you can as fast as you can and keep your percentage high. In our early years at eBay, we would not give feedback to a customer unless he or she gave it to us first. Most sellers make this same mistake. Once we started leaving feedback for customers as soon as they paid for an item, our feedback started to grow quickly. As our feedback grew, so did our sales. We now consistently sell some items at higher prices than our competitors simply because we have a high rating and take care of our customers.
>
> —mcpricebreakers

- feedback you've received has obscene, racist, or vulgar language.
- feedback you've received reveals your personal information, such as your home address.
- buyer has bid on your items for the sole purpose of leaving negative feedback.

In these instances you are encouraged to contact eBay for their help. In most other instances, you're left to your own devices.

## *Don't Fight Fire with Fire*

Sellers have the ability to respond to negative feedback that they feel is unwarranted. If you choose to respond to negative feedback you have received, and you should, don't use it as a way to fight back. Remain calm and stick to the facts of the matter. For example, if you get burned with negative feedback for late shipping, but you stated clearly in your auction that shipping would be delayed for this item, simply make a note of that underneath the negative feedback. For example:

Neg: *Seller waited five days before shipping out my monitor!*

Reply: *Delayed ship date was clearly stated in item description for duration of auction.*

Try to remain calm, factual, and emotionless. The potential bidders who read your feedback comments will appreciate your cool-headed professionalism.

CHAPTER 9

# Starting a **Business**

STARTING ANY BUSINESS, WHETHER IT IS BASED ON eBay or not, requires careful planning. Before you invest the family savings in a thousand motherboards or ink jet cartridges, you should sit down and think through your upcoming adventure. There are many things to consider. In this chapter, we'll cover the most important things to think about, and then provide you with some places to find help when you need it.

## Finances

There are two ways to go about building your business financially. You can start small, using some extra personal funds to buy inventory, and then slowly build your inventory and subsequent sales as you begin collecting profits. Or, you could seek out a bank loan to help you stock your shelves and begin your business with more sales and faster turnover.

Building your business slowly is the safer option financially because of the low start-up costs. Though it requires time, patience, and a lot of work in addition to your day job. This method also gives your competition the ability to beat you on price. When you are first starting out, you'll need to buy from your item sources in small quantities, which is often more expensive per item than buying in large quantities. Larger sellers who are able to buy large quantities for the discounts are then able to offer their items at lower prices. Their higher sales volume will also produce more revenue (and profits) for them per month, making it even easier for them to buy in large quantities.

The main benefit to starting slowly is that you'll be free of debt. Starting a business without a loan gives you the freedom to grow at your own pace, take time off if necessary, and even pull the plug if you decide that selling on eBay isn't for you.

Taking out a loan could make your start-up easier. You will be able to buy inventory in larger quantities, sell more items, and for lower prices, making competing with other sellers easier initially. However, getting the loan itself will be challenging. Banks do not pass out money to start-ups. In fact, most banks will not provide your business with a loan unless you have already established reliable item sources, a solid customer base, and a proven track record of profits that prove your business's ability to make payments on the loan. These requirements sometimes make it hard for start-ups to find financing. But there are options.

If you feel confident in your business, you might consider taking out a personal loan or a second mortgage on your home. This is considerably more risky than a business loan because, if your business fails, you stand to lose your house and income in one blow. Also, because it is a personal loan, you will still owe the bank long after the business is gone. So, if you decide to take this route, be sure that you have done all the planning and anticipation that you can, right down to the smallest detail. The following sections list some things to consider.

## Business Types

For tax purposes you will need to define your business to the Internal Revenue Service (IRS). There are several types of business classifications to choose from, each with benefits and drawbacks. Choose the one that best suits your intentions.

### Sole Proprietorship

A sole proprietorship is the most common type of start-up business because it requires little paperwork. You are the only owner. Legally, financially, and tax-wise there is no difference between you and your business. Your business's assets are your assets. Your business debt is your personal debt. And your business's profits are your income.

The advantage to this type of business is that it is easy to start and you keep all the profits for yourself. You need only to file a business income form (Schedule C) along with your regular taxes. The disadvantage of this type of business is that you are personally liable for all the business's debt and mistakes. If your business is sued for any reason, you are directly sued.

## *Partnership*

A partnership is similar to a sole proprietorship, except instead of one proprietor, there are two. Both parties are legally and financially responsible for the business. Some partnerships are based on common interests (such as husband-wife teams) and some are based on financial need (such as the financier and the manager).

If you're interested in setting up a partnership, be sure to be excruciatingly clear going in to the business about who takes on what role, who makes what decisions, and who receives what money. A clearly defined relationship will go a long way toward making the business relationship a success.

## *Corporation*

Unlike a sole proprietorship or partnership, a corporation is its own legal entity. A corporation's debt, taxes, profits, and legal liability are separate from the corporate owner. Though this provides immense protections for owners, corporations can be tricky and expensive to get started, and is therefore not often the first choice of start-up businesses. If you're interested in starting a corporation, you should contact an attorney in your area for help.

### S Corporations

An S corporation provides tax benefits to owners. Instead of taxing owners twice like corporations do, once as corporate income tax and once on owner dividends, an S corporation doesn't pay taxes on its corporate income. Owners only pay taxes on their own income from the S corporation. S corporations also offer all the same legal and financial protections that corporations do, so this may be a smarter choice for your start-up.

### Limited Liability Corporation

Like an S corporation, Limited Liability Corporations (LLCs) provide owners with legal and financial protection, while avoiding the double taxation that occurs in corporations. This is quickly becoming the default choice for small businesses. Setting up an LLC is relatively easy as well. Talk to your local chamber of commerce or SCORE chapter about where to find the necessary forms.

## Registering Your Business Name

In many states it is necessary for you to register your business name, sometimes called a "fictitious name," with the state before you can do such things as open a business bank account or apply for a bank loan. Registering your business name also ensures that you have the rights to that name in your state. Other companies will still be able to operate under your registered name, but if it ever came to a legal battle, you would have claim. Registration is a simple process that involves a simple form, a small processing fee, and a stamp. Check with your state's Small Business Administration web site for more information.

## Inventory Issues

Buying your inventory can be seen as the "no-turning-back" point. Once you've made such a large investment, you're committed to making the business work. That's why it is important to take care of your inventory as closely as you would if it were the actual cash equivalent.

### *Storage*

Your inventory must be stored safely in an appropriate facility. All computer equipment and accessories, due to the fragile electric components, require a dry and clean storage area. Cardboard boxes must be kept up off the concrete floor to prevent shock and moisture damage. Your inventory must also be stored in a manner that makes it easy to retrieve the items you need without moving a bunch of boxes around to get to them. Continuously moving boxes of fragile equipment will, over time, destroy your inventory.

Many PowerSellers who started their businesses in their basements quickly realized that the damp, dark, soggy conditions are less than ideal for their needs. Before long these sellers were able to rent storage facilities in the less-expensive industrial areas around their towns. The low rents and large facilities suit their businesses perfectly. They have plenty of space to store their inventories, plenty of room for their shipping departments, and plenty of room for the FedEx or UPS trucks to back up to the loading docks. A fancy and expensive Main Street store front is not required as all of their selling occurs online. Before you make the investment in inventory, be sure that you have arranged for the proper facilities to receive, manage, store, and ship that inventory.

## *Materials*

In addition to investing in your inventory, you will need to make an investment in supplies for your business. You will obviously need a computer, though a computer capable of loading eBay can be found quite inexpensively these days. You will need shipping materials that are appropriate for the items you will be shipping. Computers require a lot of protection. A bumpy road, dropped box, or a simple static shock could render the item useless to the buyer. As the seller, it is your responsibility to make sure that the item is packed in such a way that it can withstand a reasonable amount of abuse while in transit.

Many sellers who build custom computers use the box and padding that was used to ship the computer case. They simply build the computer, repackage the case into its original box, and ship a complete computer that way. If you are buying parts in bulk, you will likely not have the luxury of individual boxes delivered directly to you. If that's the case you will need to purchase shipping boxes and materials. Choose a box that is at least three inches larger on every side than the item you're shipping. Pack the box full of some sort of padding like foam peanuts, foam blocks, or air bags. Wrap the entire item in a clear, sealed plastic bag for protection before plunging it into the peanuts. In some cases a static-free bag should be used, as foam peanuts tend to be great little generators of static electricity.

You can find all these items on eBay. Savvy sellers have realized that one of the largest markets on eBay is, in fact, other sellers. And therefore packing and shipping materials are quite easy to find at great prices all over eBay. If you're in a rush and don't want to wait a few days for delivery, try your local Staples, Office Depot, UPS Store, or U-Haul supply store. They all generally have adequate packing and shipping departments.

CHAPTER 10

# Tools to Help
# You Work Smarter

AN INDUSTRY IS GROWING TO AID EBAY SELLERS. Research, software, and consulting companies are being created every day to help sellers sell. As a result, many tools are available to you to make selling easier, faster, and more cost efficient. Even eBay itself provides many tools to help you along. In this chapter, we'll cover some of eBay's tools and some of the third-party solutions that are available to help you reach PowerSeller status.

To help sellers discover even more helpful tools, eBay has created a directory full of third-party solutions. Visit the directory by clicking the Solutions Directory link on the left side of eBay's main page.

## Research Tools

Choosing the correct items to sell is a key factor to your business's success. To help you make an informed decision, companies have released the following research tools. Be sure to take advantage of at least one of these services before you begin selling in earnest.

### eBay Pulse

eBay Pulse, at http://pulse.ebay.com, will provide you with some general information about the current popular trends in eBay buying and selling. Choose Computers & Networking from the pull-down menu to find the latest trends in the category. This simple page will tell you the most popular computer category searches, the largest computer stores, and the most watched computer items. This information changes every day, and is therefore a good thing to keep an eye on. Click through the top searches to find top selling items for that particular search term. Is there anything in there that you might like to sell? Who is selling the most of these items? Can you find ways to do it better? Browse through the largest stores to find out what they've got to offer. eBay Pulse is a great place to begin thinking about what the hot items are in the computer category, and what you would like to begin selling.

### Marketplace Research

eBay also offers a service called Marketplace Research. This tool provides a place for sellers to do in-depth research about the items they are, or hope to begin, selling. Sellers can find up to 90 days of completed listing information, as opposed to the usual 30 days available through Advanced Search; top searches in a particular category or across the whole site; average sale and average start price for any given item, and many other tools.

There are three subscription levels: Fast Pass, Basic, and Pro. Fast Pass is a nonrenewing two-day subscription for $2.99. Basic and Pro are monthly subscriptions that can be had for $9.99 and $24.99 respectively. You can view the details of Marketplace Research and the services offered to the different subscription levels at http://pages.ebay.com/marketplace_research.

This service receives mixed reviews from sellers. Some complain that it is over priced and is limited in its services, whereas many others applaud the service as being helpful and thorough. Visit the Marketplace Research discussion board to read some reviews before taking the plunge. In our experience it has been quite helpful for quick research, though limited in its offerings compared to the more established eBay research companies.

## *Terapeak.com*

Terapeak.com's Marketplace Research tool is similar to eBay's Marketplace Research tool in that it allows you to research market trends, item performance, buyer habits, and more for any given item or category. Terapeak is well regarded as an easy-to-use and effective service that has been helping eBay sellers since 2003. It is an online tool and requires no software download. The service has two subscription levels: Research Lite for $9.95 per month, or Research Complete for $16.95 per month or $169.50 per year.

### Andale

Andale is the most well-known eBay market research company. They have been around almost since the inception of eBay itself. Their research tool is called, appropriately, Andale Research. It is a web-based tool, thereby avoiding the problems of operating system-specific programs, and is the lowest priced at only $7.95 per month.

Andale Research can tell you much of the same information as the other services, such as item and category information. But it will also provide you with a recommendation for what time of the day and week to list your item for maximum profitability; a comparison of an item's eBay selling price compared to retail selling prices on Froogle, Shopping.com, and BizRate. It will also tell you which type of listing (auction, Buy It Now, etc.) will get you the best price for your item.

In addition to the market research tools, Andale offers a whole line of services to help the eBay seller, such as Sales Analyzer to help you get maximum profit from your existing listings, and Andale Supplier, a tool to help you find the best source for the items you sell.

### HammerTap's DeepAnalysis 2

HammerTap offers quite a few services to help the eBay seller. Their market research tool, DeepAnalysis 2, is a software download. It helps sellers find out what is selling by analyzing data and providing reports about specific eBay sellers, categories, items, and keywords. DeepAnalysis 2 not only helps sellers find out what is selling, but why. It finds the average starting price, auction length, and the payment types accepted for items that are selling the most reliably. You can use this information to fine tune your listings for better sales. DeepAnalysis 2 is a robust tool with many ways to help a seller, only a fraction of which we're able to cover here. It does, however, have some drawbacks. It is fairly expensive at $17.95 per month, and runs only on Windows, leaving out Mac and Linux users. Take advantage of the free trial and judge for yourself.

## Auction Management Tools

Submitting every auction via eBay's web site would be clunky, time consuming, and visually painful. PowerSellers could not have become PowerSellers if they spent all their time listing individual auctions through eBay's web site. Therefore, to facilitate listing more than a few products per month, many companies have created software that helps sellers list, duplicate, re-list, and manage their auctions. The following sections list a few that are commonly used by PowerSellers.

### eBay's Tools

eBay provides a few tools to help sellers better manage their auctions. They include:

- *TurboLister*, a bulk listing tool with HTML templates.
- *Selling Manager*, an online auction management tool that includes feedback templates, bulk relisting, invoicing, downloadable sales history, and bulk feedback. Best when used in conjunction with TurboLister.
- *Selling Manager Pro*, an online auction management tool that includes inventory management, listing statistics, bulk feedback and invoicing, automated e-mails, and more.
- *Blackthorne Basic*, a download application for PCs that helps sellers create listings, manage auctions, and manage customer correspondence.
- *Blackthorne Pro*, a download application for PCs that is a complete auction management tool. It creates listings, manages auctions, manages customer correspondence, handles bulk processing, and helps with post-auction tasks, such as invoicing.

## Auctiva

Auctiva is a free tool that helps sellers create listings, schedule auctions, cross-market auctions, host images, manage sales, generate reports, and increase efficiency. It is an online tool. To learn more, or to sign up, visit www.auctiva.com.

## ChannelAdvisor

ChannelAdvisor offers all levels of service from helping you manage your first few auctions, to helping large corporations liquidate entire companies. Their auction management software is ChannelAdvisor Pro. It is a web-based tool that offers templates for your listings, image hosting, inventory management capabilities, customer correspondence, and post-auction checkout. One of the benefits of ChannelAdvisor is the many levels of service they provide. You will not outgrow their services. For more information, visit www.channeladvisor.com.

## Photo Hosting Services

To become a PowerSeller you will need to display as many photos of your items as you

> We soon found out that we needed automation to expand our eBay business. Within only a month of selling on eBay we started looking to automate. We found Truition, at www.truition.com. Their online CMS software, which handles inventory control, listing on eBay, checkout, collecting payments, automatic e-mailing of customers, and automatic feedback, has fully automated our eBay business.
>
> —goodasnewcomputerscanada

can. Research shows that there is direct relationship between the number of photos in an auction and the final sale price. Simply stated, buyers want to see what they're buying, and the more you can show to them, the more likely they are to make the purchase. If you stick with eBay's photo services, adding more photos means adding to the listing price, and when you are listing several thousand items a month, a difference of 45 cents per item will add up fast. To avoid those per-photo fees, you can use one of these photo hosting services listed in the following section and then link to the photos in your auctions description with a simple HTML tag. Your auction will be able to display as many photos you would like at no incremental cost.

### FotoTime

For only $23.95 per year, FotoTime provides enough storage for you to have thousands of photos online. They also provide thumbnail versions of each photo you upload for convenient placement into your auction pages. For more information, go to www.fototime.com.

### VillagePhotos

VillagePhoto has many different photo hosting plans for you to choose from. They offer low prices and useful options such as a browser uploading tool, a photo album for easy management, and automatic thumbnails. If you plan to grow beyond eBay into other online marketplaces, VillagePhotos also integrates well with Yahoo! Auctions and Yahoo! Stores. Their plans start at just $3.95 per month. For more information, visit www.villagephotos.com.

### Photobucket.com

Photobucket.com is a free online photo hosting and album service. They have an online uploading tool, photo manager, a public photo album feature, and easy eBay integration. They also integrate well with other web sites such as myspace.com and other blog sites.

These are just some of the tools that help sellers. If you can't find what you need here, visit eBay's Solution Directory for hundreds of more programs. Also, you can visit www.auctionsoftwarereview.com for an independent source of auction management software downloads and reviews.

CHAPTER 11

# Advanced Marketing **Strategies**

SINCE IT'S LAUNCH IN 1995, EBAY HAS GROWN TO become exactly what it touts itself to be: The World's Online Marketplace. In the early days, marketing was not much of a concern for sellers, simply listing items for auction was enough. But today, due to the astronomical growth in the number of auctions running at any given time, losing your auctions in the crowd is a distinct possibility. Today, marketing is a must. If you are not taking steps to attract large numbers of bidders to your auctions, they will be overshadowed. Your sales rates will suffer along with your final sale price. Fortunately, there are relatively simple steps you can take to ensure that interested buyers find your auction. I've outlined some of the strategies employed by PowerSellers in the following sections.

## Marketing within eBay

Once the framework of your business has been established, it is time to turn your attention to getting the attention of buyers. As mentioned earlier, the more bidders you can attract the better. The following information will help you to attract and maintain your bidders.

### Timing Your Auctions

An auction is most visible when it is in its final few minutes. eBay's listing sort order defaults to "Time: ending soonest," and therefore the auctions with the least time remaining rise to the top of the page. Most buyers never bother to re-sort the listing to anything other than the default, and therefore the overwhelming majority of bidders who see your auction see it in its final few minutes. So, naturally, you benefit by aligning those final few minutes of your auction with eBay's peak traffic times. This makes the time when your auction is most visible also the time when there are the most bidders on eBay.

The conventional wisdom, as mentioned in Chapter 5, is that Sunday nights between the

> We have found that ending our auctions at night works best. Our selling price is higher when the item ends between 8 P.M. and 11 P.M.
> 
> —goodasnewcomputerscanada

hours of 6 P.M. and midnight (EST) are eBay's peak traffic hours. In our own research we found that over 50 percent of PowerSellers asked claimed Sunday to be the most successful day to end an auction. Monday was a distant second with only 10 percent of the vote.

There are two ways to end an auction during peak hours. You could manually submit your auction during that time and set the auction's duration for seven days. Though, if you have more than a few auctions to submit, this process will be time consuming and slow given the high-traffic on eBay's site during this time. Or, you could simply pay eBay the additional 10 cents per listing and schedule your auctions to begin during this time slot with a seven-day duration. Also, some of the auction management software we outlined in Chapter 10 allows you to schedule listings. There are fees associated with doing it via these programs as well, though the more expensive ones integrate the scheduling costs into your monthly fee.

> We like to end auctions during late evening hours and on weekends, although we do end some auctions during the workday as well. Many buyers appear to be individuals who are browsing and buying in their free time. Perhaps after work or after the kids are in bed. We have seen a gradual increase in people buying during the workday. These buyers are typically buying for their own business use or for sale to their clients.
>
> —somersetsales

## Teaser Auctions

Now that you've got your auctions timed to maximize exposure, you can begin guiding traffic into your auctions, fixed-price listings, and eBay store with teaser auctions. A teaser auction is set up just like a regular auction, but using a highly popular item, a low starting price, and cross-promotion. The Cross-Promotion tool is available to eBay store owners and places thumbnails of items you've selected from your store into all of your auctions, thereby advertising your more profitable items to interested bidders. These teaser auctions are designed to show up in the main site's search results listings to capture the attention of bidders traveling eBay's main traffic stream.

## Featured Listings

When you can afford to, take advantage of eBay's Featured Listings promotional tools. These are expensive, but when used with your eBay store and the Cross-Promotion tool, are highly effective at driving a lot of bidders to your store and auctions. Always use your best-selling items in these Featured auctions, and make sure that the products you've chosen to cross-promote are directly related to the Featured auction's item. Bidders will not follow a link to an item in which they have no interest. Also, as these will be your most prominent auctions, be sure to spell check your text, proofread, and double check your photos for clarity and accuracy. It is important that these highly visible auctions reflect your business well.

## E-Mail Marketing

Included in your eBay store subscription is an E-mail Marketing tool that allows your customers to subscribe to your eBay Store newsletter. An e-mail newsletter can be a great way to promote sales, specials, your store, and your auctions. The E-mail Marketing tool lets you manage up to five e-mail lists so you can customize your newsletters to your buyers' specific interests.

By doing business on eBay you will be in constant contact with your customers via e-mail. Even if you choose not to use your eBay Store E-mail Marketing tool, it would be a good idea to begin building a database of the e-mail addresses of your customers. Keep careful notes about what each person has purchased from you for appropriate sorting later.

As mentioned earlier, eBay has a strict no-spamming rule that you need to adhere to when putting together e-mail campaigns. You must ask your customers if they would like to subscribe to your mailing list before you begin sending out e-mails and provide them with a way to opt out if they agree. If you use your eBay Store's E-mail Marketing tool, this will be taken care of for you. If you plan to collect and market to e-mail addresses on your own, get permission first.

## Correspondence Promotion

Every time you have contact with a customer, you are presented with an opportunity to do a little promotion. In every package you ship, insert a flier advertising an upcoming sale or new product line. On every invoice you print, include the address to your eBay store or make a note about the other popular items you sell. In every e-mail you send out, whether it is a winner confirmation, a payment request, or a post-auction follow-up, include a link to your eBay store. These simple steps are inexpensive, but will help you spread the word about your business in big ways. Always be looking for new promotional ideas.

## Marketing Outside eBay

Many successful PowerSellers have their own web site. Some use it as a complete e-commerce site separate from eBay, but most find that juggling inventories for two sites is more trouble than it is worth. Your own web site, whether you choose to sell items from it or not, can be a valuable promotional tool for your eBay auctions and store.

Searches in the major search engines, such as Google and Yahoo!, will not often produce results from within eBay. Therefore your eBay store, your auctions, and products cannot be easily found through major search engines. This is a large problem that is, luckily, easily corrected. With a simple independent web site that advertises your eBay store, you can open up your business to the millions of search engine users that would otherwise never see your business. And, by sending customers directly from search engines to your web site to your eBay store, you can cleverly route them right past all your eBay competition.

## Promotional Programs

Once you have your own web site, you will be able to take advantage of off-eBay promotional services such as Google's AdWords program and Overture's marketing tools. These can significantly increase traffic to your web site and to your eBay auctions and store.

As an additional bonus, eBay recognizes that any off-eBay promotion of your store that you do also promotes eBay as a whole. Therefore, they offer sellers who market their stores off-eBay a 75 percent Final Value Fees discount through the Stores Referral Credit program. See the eBay Stores tutorial pages for more information.

## Traditional Real-World Advertising

Don't underestimate the power of traditional, real-world advertising strategies. When used in combination with your own independent web site, placing advertisements in computer trade magazines, on public transportation, and in local newspapers can be quite effective. Advertise your products and your web address just as you would for any other "real" business, because, after all, you have a real business. You'll be attracting market segments that most eBay sellers, and internet businesses in general, rarely think to reach out to.

CHAPTER 12

# Inventory Management

THERE ARE TWO WAYS TO HANDLE THE ITEMS YOU SELL on eBay. You can purchase the items outright and stock them in your warehouse or storage facility yourself, or you can avoid handling inventory all together by finding sources that offer drop-shipping. In this chapter, we'll cover the benefits of both methods so that you can decide which is best for you before you get started.

## Drop-Shipping

Drop-shipping is a shipping option that some manufacturers, retailers, and distributors offer to resellers to streamline the selling process. Resellers that use drop-shipping never touch their products. Instead, they simply notify the shipping department at the item's source company when an item is purchased, and the item is then shipped directly from the source to the customer. This leaves the reseller free to deal with marketing, auction management, customer service, and payment collection without having to set up inventory management or a shipping department.

Though drop-shipping may sound like the ideal shipping solution for eBay sellers, it does have significant drawbacks. First, surrendering control over the shipping of the items you sell puts you entirely at the mercy of the source company. If they run out of stock, or are delayed in shipping, or even fail to ship an item, it will be a difficult process for you to get things straightened out with them and then make things right with your customer.

Second, the number of companies that offer drop-shipping is limited, therefore, your options of what to sell are limited. Your decision about what items to sell should be based on profitability and popularity, not on available shipping options.

Finally, if your product line consists of items from only one or two sources and both sources offer drop-shipping, then it might not be a bad idea for you to take advantage of it. However, if you seek to expand your product line in the future, you could end up trying to manage drop-shipments from ten or more companies. This can grow to become so unwieldy and unmanageable that the thought of centralizing all your products and shipments in your own single warehouse may begin to appeal to you.

## Taking on Inventory

If you've made the decision that drop-shipping isn't your cup of tea, then you've got some planning ahead of you. The first step is finding the finances to make the initial investment in inventory. The second step is finding a storage or warehouse location that meets your needs. And finally you will need to put together a comprehensive strategy for taking care of all your new goodies.

Proper inventory management is essential to any eBay seller's business. When buying and selling thousands of items per week, tracking inventory from source to shelves to shipment can be a monumental task. Many eBay businesses experience growing pains in this area because as their sales increase, they neglect to upgrade their internal inventory management and end up selling items twice, shipping items that haven't sold, and even selling items they haven't yet purchased. These mistakes disappoint customers and quickly tarnish otherwise radiant feedback ratings. Before you start stocking your shelves, be sure that the inventory management strategy you have in place is sufficient for your current needs and will grow along with you.

### Space Concerns

Your inventory storage facility must be large enough to hold your inventory comfortably, furnish a shipping department, a photography area, store extra shipping supplies, and allow room for growth. If you are planning to sell just a few items a month, this space might be only as large as the corner of your dining room. Many first-rate eBay businesses have started this way. However, as soon as you begin to develop regular sales, you'll need a facility more suited to your business needs.

Computers, networking equipment, and other electronic accessories have special needs. They are highly sensitive to their environment, and therefore you need to find, or build, a dry space with relatively ambient temperatures and plenty of shelf space. Self-storage units are sometimes used because they offer security, climate-control, and a low initial expense. However, they can sometimes be difficult to access after business hours, they don't leave much room for growth, and they often don't allow you to schedule regular shipping pick-ups from UPS or FedEx.

If you live in the city or suburbs, look around the industrial parks in your area. You may be able to rent a garage bay with ideal shipping capabilities for not too much more than a self-storage unit. Low-rent "behind-the-scenes" business parks make ideal locations for an eBay business. If you are out in rural locations, look around for some space in a local barn or warehouse.

## *Software*

In Chapter 10 we outlined some auction management programs. All of these programs will help you track your auctions, from listing to sale to feedback. Though, some of them, such as ChannelAdvisor Pro, will also help you to track the flow of your inventory. A good program will notify you when stock of a particular item is running low, will either relist or restock items that failed to sell at auction, and will track your item sources and source expenses.

## Layout

If you have the luxury of laying out the floor plan of your storage facility, consider "flow." The best spaces allow for a continuous stream of inventory through the various stages of handling: logging new inventory, testing (if necessary), photography, shelving, and shipping.

> We use MYOB to manage our inventory—can't beat it.
> —mcpricebreakers
>
> *Author's note*: MYOB Limited publishes software to help small businesses manage common tasks. They offer programs for both the Mac and Windows platforms. To learn more visit www.myob.com.

If you have two bay doors, make one "in" for incoming inventory from your item sources, and make one "out" for shipments to customers. If you have only one bay door, send all incoming item shipments directly to a processing area where they are logged into the management software, assigned an inventory ID code, and checked for accuracy and damage. Next, if you're dealing with used computer equipment, shuffle it all to your testing area where you can make sure everything functions properly. Then, pass everything on to photography where the photos that you will need to use in your auctions are taken. If your auction management software doesn't already do this for you, create a photo database to keep track of which photos correspond with what items. For this purpose, have a networked computer set up at the photography station to make your job of listing auctions easier later. Once everything is photographed, you can stock it on your storage shelves while it awaits auction. Label your shelving system and stock your items according to the inventory ID that each item has been assigned, or by a similar cataloging system, so that when it comes time to ship an item, it will be easily located. Once an item has sold, send it off to the shipping department, and out the "out" door to the happy customer.

In the example above, managing a warehouse such as this sounds like enough work for a team of people. And while, ideally, it would be, many eBay sellers must make do with much less. To further organize the process and maximize the work of one or two people, many PowerSellers assign a specific task to different days of the week. For example, on Sunday they devote the day to creating and submitting new auctions to eBay. On Monday, to ensure fast shipping to the customers, they pack and ship all the items that have sold in the auctions that ended on Sunday. On Tuesday, they search for, and purchase, their inventory from the usual sources. On Wednesday, they log in and check all the new inventory shipments that have arrived at the warehouse since last Wednesday. On Thursday, they do the necessary photography, and on Friday they stock the items onto the warehouse shelves. Saturday might be a day off, but more likely, the day will be spent doing everything they couldn't finish up during the week. Of course, this schedule makes for a hectic week, but on the bare-bones budget of a new business, sometimes it is necessary.

## Shipping

There are three main companies that sellers choose to handle their shipping: UPS, FedEx, or the U.S. Postal Service. You will have to research which company works best for you in your area and location. The U.S. Postal Service tends to be the least expensive, but you'll need to deliver packages to the post office every time you ship. UPS and FedEx are a little pricier, but will come to your door to pick up shipments. All three provide tracking numbers for your packages, which buyers always appreciate having. When shipping internationally, be sure to fill out all the appropriate customs forms from whichever company you choose.

CHAPTER 13

# Finances

**W**ITH THE POSSIBILITY OF HUNDREDS OF TRANSACTIONS per month, you will need to be diligent about tracking and recording your business's finances. Not only will solid accounting practices help you come tax time, they will also help you secure a bank loan, evaluate the health of your business, and prove necessary when it comes time to sell the company.

There are several ways to manage your business's finances. You could take on the responsibility yourself, doing it either by hand or in accounting software, or you could hire an accountant to help you. If you're confident in your bookkeeping skills and have the time and energy to take on the task yourself, then by all means, you should. However, you shouldn't take on your own bookkeeping if you're not sure of yourself, if you don't have adequate time to do the job, or if you're just trying to save a few bucks. Doing a lousy job of bookkeeping will no doubt cost you more in the end than simply hiring an accountant up front.

## Doing It Yourself

If you decide to take on the job yourself, you can easily find formidable help in the form of accounting software. There are a few great programs available that are designed to do exactly what you need. Luckily, if you accept most of your payments from buyers through PayPal, you will have easy access to a downloadable record of your received payments, which you can plug into the accounting software you choose. Also, if your auction management software allows you to track inventory, you should be able to export a list of all your inventory purchases as well. These two lists combine to compile an already formidable record of your business's finances. All you need to do is fill in around the edges with information such as your office and shipping expenses, income received from outside (non-PayPal) sources, rent, utilities, and so on.

Research the following programs before you decide to depend on one. Some have downloadable demo versions that will allow you to evaluate the software for a period of time.

## QuickBooks

Perhaps most well known is the business accounting program QuickBooks, from Intuit, the makers of Quicken. QuickBooks is available for both Mac and PCs, costs between $100 and $400 depending on the version, and releases an upgrade every year to stay current with tax information. For more information, visit www.quickbooks.com.

## Money, Small Business

Microsoft's Money for small business is another widely used financial management application. It will help you manage your accounts, your spending, and your profit and loss reports through a simple interface. Money only runs on Windows XP or higher PCs and costs around $90. For more information, visit www.microsoft.com/money.

## PeachTree

PeachTree's small business accounting software has been around and popular for many years. It is a robust accounting program specifically designed for small businesses. It, like Money, only operates on Windows PCs. It costs $199.95 and releases a new version every year. For more information, visit www.peachtree.com.

# Business Vital Signs

The most important aspect of doing your own bookkeeping is to actually do it. Saving all your receipts and invoices for a rainy day during tax season will not help you to produce the quarterly, monthly, and weekly reports that you will need to make smart business decisions. You should be aware at all times of your company's vital signs, as indicated by your profit and loss statement, cash flow statement, and balance sheet.

Your profit and loss statement (P&L) should be easily produced from within your accounting software. It is simply a record of all your income and expenses over a given time period, usually a month. It will let you know whether your business is profitable and, if not, where you need to make changes. Keep a file of previous months' P&Ls so that you can compare and track whether the changes you've made are working.

A cash flow statement simply tracks the money that comes into and goes out of your business. It can be used to track where your cash has gone, and to predict where your cash will be down the road. You should create a cash flow statement often enough that you are never side-swiped by surprises. You need to know that you will have enough cash available to purchase next month's inventory. Otherwise, you'll be left with nothing to sell and no income.

A balance sheet measures all your assets (inventory, vehicles, cash, accounts receivable, etc.) against all your liabilities (loans, rent, accounts payable, etc.) and determines what your business is worth. Keeping a close eye on this report will let you know if your business is growing, or headed for failure. Generate this often for early signs of trouble.

## Finding Help

You have quite enough to stay on top of without trying to remain current on all the latest tax laws. Your time will be better spent watching for trends and innovations on eBay than watching for the latest IRS tax codes. Accountants can relieve you of a lot of stress, and therefore you should consider passing your accounting on to one of them.

Talk to other local businesses to find out who they trust for their accounting. If that search turns up empty, talk to your local SCORE chapter, your chamber of commerce, or your state's Small Business Administration for recommendations. You'll want to interview several accountants before you enlist the help of one. Be sure to inquire into her work history. Has she been in the profession long? Is she a Certified Public Accountant? How much experience does she have accounting for small businesses? Solicit resumes, ask for references, and then follow through on calling them all. Your business will profit from your diligent research.

CHAPTER 14

# Human
# Resources

*T*HE DAY WILL COME WHEN IT IS NECESSARY FOR YOU to start hiring employees. This chapter will discuss how to know when that day has arrived and what steps to take when it does. It will be a busy day, no doubt, and you likely will feel stressed and anxious about taking the time to find help amid your already hectic schedule. But take a deep breath and relax. This is a necessary and exciting step to building a business. Once you've got good employees behind you, your business will really start to take off.

## When to Hire

Running an eBay business takes a lot of work. It requires long hours in front of a computer screen, a lot of time on the phone, and some stressful financial decisions. It is indeed a full-time job. But it should only be a full-time job. When the number of hours you work in a week creeps past 40 to 50 to 60 and worse, you should consider hiring some help. Remember, you started this eBay business to have more fun, take control of your schedule, and to free up some time. Didn't you?

If you find yourself working over 40 hours a week to keep up with the demands of the business you should be in a position financially to afford one or two part-time employees. If you're not in a position to take on a few salaries, you should reassess the profitability of your business. Would it be more profitable to run less auctions at higher prices? Or, would the extra help be all that you needed to increase sales and cover the salaries? In either case, you should speak with your accountant about taking on help. He will be able to help you determine how much you can afford to pay, and whether you should offer benefits.

## Before You Hire

Prior to hiring employees there are things you must do. New employees means new planning and new paperwork. The first step before you hire is to get yourself set up properly with the government.

## Employer Identification Number

Up until this point, if you have operated your business as a sole-proprietorship, you have not needed an Employer Identification Number (EIN). An EIN is to a business what a social security number is to an individual. It simply identifies your business to the IRS and will be used when you withhold income taxes from your employee paychecks. To apply for your EIN, you will need to fill out, and submit, IRS Form SS-4. It can be downloaded from www.irs.gov/pub/irs-pdf/fss4.pdf.

## Planning for Employees

Before you begin interviewing you should figure out where another set of hands would be most effective. What is the most time-consuming task in your day? Is it easily delegated to someone else or does it require your expertise? If you find yourself spending six hours a day shipping orders, you might consider hiring someone to take that on and free yourself up to generate more income for the business. Your time is best spent working on your business, not in it.

A helpful tool you can create is an employee map of your business. Draw out a job tree, placing yourself at the top as the boss. Below you, sketch the branches of your company: auction management, customer service, accounting, inventory management, shipping, and others. Within the branches, map out the individual jobs that you would need to make each branch run effectively. For each job you've mapped out, write a clear job description.

It may be years before your business is able to fill all the positions you've planned. But now is the time to begin filling them. Start with the jobs that can be easily filled and would most effectively free up your time. Then, work toward filling the ones that aren't as crucial but would make everything run more smoothly. In the beginning, you may need to hire one person for a few positions. But, because you've already written clear job descriptions, you can simply hand your new employee two or three descriptions and divide his week up accordingly.

### Finding Employees

Finding people to apply for the positions you've created might be the easiest step in the whole process. Place an ad in your local papers, talk to friends and relatives, or put up fliers at the mall. Once you begin advertising your position, applicants will come find you. Be aware of the markets in which you're advertising. If you're looking for an accountant, fliers at the mall will likely not yield legitimate results. If you're looking for a teenager to help part-time with auction listings, advertising accordingly.

### Screening Applicants

One of the largest problem areas for small business owners is troublesome employees. This is your chance to do all you can to weed out the potentially troublesome employees before you begin hiring. In addition to accepting the standard employment application—available at any local office supply store—make sure you also check references, proof of citizenship, conduct interviews, and do background checks. Hiring help will not help your business any if you end up with a thief in the middle of your stock room. Conversely, hiring the right people now may be exactly what your business needs to grow to the next level.

## After You Hire

Now that you've got employees, your business is ready to roll. Or is it? There are still a few concerns that need your attention. Simply filling positions will not help a company run. Now you need to make sure your employees know what they're here to do, and you need to know what to do to take care of them.

### More Paperwork

In addition to keeping your new employee's application, resume (if submitted), and references on file, you also need to collect some tax information from them. As the employer, you will be withholding income tax on your employee's paychecks. The amount you withhold is determined by the information your employee fills out on his or her Form W-4. You will need to keep a copy of Form W-4, and mail one off to the IRS.

You must also ask your new employee to fill out Form I-9, the Employment Eligibility Verification. To do this you will need a copy of the employee's passport, or driver's license and social security card. For a complete list of acceptable forms of identification, see the back of Form I-9. You must keep every employee's Form I-9 on file for a period of three years from the hiring date. This form is not mailed to anyone.

## Training

Spending time thoroughly training your new employee may seem like a nuisance and distraction now, but it will pay off for you in the long run. It is easier to train an employee well in the first two weeks than it is to be pulled away to help out your help every few minutes for six months. Provide your employee with the detailed job description you wrote out at the beginning of this process. She will find it a useful guide when she has questions.

## Taxes

**FEDERAL INCOME TAX.** As mentioned above, you need to withhold federal income taxes from your employees on every paycheck. The appropriate amount to withhold is determined by the tax information the individual employee supplies on his Form W-4. Use this information to find the appropriate amount in IRS Publication 15, *Circular E, Employer's Tax Guide*.

**FICA.** In addition to federal income tax, you must also withhold Social Security and Medicare taxes from your employees and pay a matching amount. At the time of this writing, the Social Security tax rate is 6.2 percent for all salaries up to $76,000, and 1.45 percent for Medicare.

**FUTA.** FUTA stands for the Federal Unemployment Tax Act, and it means that you need to pay more money. You pay 6.2 percent of the first $7,000 that your employee earns. However, you receive a credit for 5.4 percent of that on your own taxes. Use Form 940 or Form 940-EZ to file these taxes.

**EMPLOYEE COMPENSATION.** Along with all the paperwork listed in the previous section, you must submit to the IRS a report of employee compensation and withholdings, along with your share of the FICA taxes, on Form 941, *Employer's Quarterly Federal Tax Return*.

When you apply for your EIN, the IRS will send you a stack of Form 8109, the *Federal Tax Deposit Coupon*. If your total quarterly employment taxes are more than $500 you will need to file these taxes using Form 8109 every month before the 15th of the following month.

At the end of the year you will need to provide your employees with their annual Form W-2s. This form, as I'm sure you know, summarizes earnings and withholdings for the year. You must deliver this form to all your employees before January 31st of the following year. You will need to keep a copy of all your employee's Form W-2s to file along with Form W-3 to the Social Security Association.

Yes, that's a lot of effort, math, and paperwork. For these reasons, many companies fill the accountant position first. If you find yourself stuck or confused by these tax requirements, you can do your own research at the following web sites:

- Social Security Administration (www.ssa.gov)
- Internal Revenue Service (www.irs.gov)
- Small Business Administration (www.sba.gov)

Or, you can find someone to help you at these sites:

- 1-800-Accountant (www.1800accountant.com)
- CPA Directory (www.cpadirectory.com)
- The National Association of Small Business Accountants (www.smallbizaccountants.com)

CHAPTER 15

# Final
# Thoughts

*W*ell, there you have it—a crash course in selling computers and computer accessories on eBay. You now know how to register on eBay, find items to sell, create effective auctions, manage inventory, and hire help when it's time! We've provided you with the best strategies for getting started, and the proven techniques for maximizing profitability. Now it's up to you to become the next successful PowerSeller in the world's largest marketplace.

As the PowerSellers, who were gracious enough to share their knowledge with us, have shown you—selling on eBay can provide you with a profitable business, or add profits to your existing business. With proper technique, good customer service, and a lot of planning, eBay's potential is limitless.

## Closing Thoughts from PowerSellers
On the possibilities eBay presents for your business:

*Our goal is that we can continue to generate sales from eBay as a sales channel, continue to grow our customer base as a result, and continue to achieve higher residual values for our used assets than if we sold them wholesale to our remarketing partners. We are also exploring our ability to buy equipment explicitly for resale on eBay, and I believe we will add bottom line profit to our company by doing this.*

—somersetsales

*In 1997 we just started placing a few items up for auction to test eBay. And, even though eBay was much smaller at the time, it soon became apparent that it would be a very lucrative avenue for sales.*

—mcpricebreakers

*I really enjoy the fact that eBay is very diverse. The market is very big and the possibilities seem endless. We could sell anything profitably if we bought it at the right price. We could sell golf balls, video games, and shoes all in the same store and be successful. Sometimes we have items that are very hard to sell through our other sales channels, but we can always sell it on eBay.*

—goodasnewcomputerscanada

On the larger benefits of the eBay Community:

*eBay puts me in contact with people around the world. It amazes me almost daily who I talk to. I've made friends from Australia to Canada. Truly wonderful!*

—chessmasterjack

*Our goal for our eBay business is really just to keep the six of us employed, and perhaps grow while keeping it fun along the way!*

—notebooksauction-dot-com

Remember, selling on eBay will not always be easy, and it will not always be fun. But you have chosen to do it because computers and technology are your passion. That fact, in itself, makes this venture more exciting than any dead-end corporate job anywhere. You have taken the reigns of your income and opened up your future to possibilities as limitless as eBay has proven, so far, to be. In time, you will learn more ins and outs of this marketplace than we could ever stuff into a pocket guide. Hopefully we've been able to set you on the right path to building a profitable business selling the items you're passionate about. I wish you the best with your new business.

# Index

**A**
*About Me* page, 22–23
Account set up, 21–26
Accountant, hiring an, 123, 133
Accounting software, 120–121
Advertising strategies, traditional real-world, 109
alienwar.com, 8–9
Andale, 96
Apple Computer, 6
apple.com, 8

Auction management tools, 97–99
Auctiva, 98
Automating your eBay business, 97–99

**B**
Bank loans, 86–87
Barton, Anthony, PowerSeller, 14–15
BestBuy, 4–5
Blackthorne Basic, 98
Blackthorne Pro, 98
Bold option, 50

Bookkeeping, 120–121
Border, adding a, 50
Boxes, shipping, 91–92
Business
   details, 2
   name, registering your, 89–90
   supplies, 91–92
   type, choosing a, 87–89
Buy it now (BIN) price, 44, 65–66
Buying smart, 35–36

**C**

Categories, 38
ChannelAdvisor, 98–99, 114
chessmasterjack, 14, 35, 52, 135
Competition
   brick-and-mortar, 4–7
   for the PowerSeller, 3–4
   online, 7–9
   researching the, 4, 9
   your, 3–10
Complaints, 81–84
   fraudulent, 82
CompUSA, 5–6
Computer parts business success, 16
Conflict resolution, 82–84
Content License clause, 19–20
Copyrights, 74–75
Corporation, forming a, 86–87

Correspondence, customer, 107–108
Cross-Promotion tool, 106
Cross-selling, 59–60
Customer
   care, 77–82
   complaints, 81–84
   conflict resolution, 82–84
   correspondence, 107–108
   during auctions, 78–80
   other eBay sellers as your potential, 92
   post-auction, 79–80
   questions, 79–80
   research, 9
   service, providing excellent, 16
   Skype, 78–79

**D**

Description, 42–43, 71–73, 78
Digital camera, 73–74
Distributors, 29–30
Donate percentage of sale, 44
Drop-shipping, 111–112
Duration of auction, 44–45

**E**

E-mail, 20–21
E-mail Marketing tool, eBay, 107
eBay Basic Picture Services, 48
eBay Pulse, 94

Employees
 compensation and withholdings, 131–132
 hiring, 126–129
 taxes, 130–131
 training, 130
End time, auction, 45–46, 104–105

**F**
Featured listings, 106
Featured Plus!, 51
FedEx, 117
Feedback
 help from eBay regarding certain kinds of, 82–83
 score, 9, 80
 sellers response to negative, 83–84
 system as double-edged sword, 2, 82–84
Final Value Fees discount, 109
Finances, 85–87, 119–123
First-time ordering, importance of customer access for, 80
FotoTime, 100
Fraud, 52, 53, 81–82

**G**
Gallery feature, 49, 51
Garage sales, 33
Gift Services, 51–52

Giving Works program, 44
goodasnewcomputers_canada, 14–15, 31, 53, 66, 99, 104, 134
Google's AdWords program, 109

**H**
HammerTap's DeepAnalysis 2, 96–97
Highlighting, 50
Hobby selling vs. PowerSelling, 2–3
Home Page Featured, 51
Human resources, 125–132

**I**
Incorporating, 86–87
Individual items, 47
Inventory
 issues, 90–91
 management, 113–117
 management software, 114–115
 resources, 27–36

**K**
Kreutzer, John, PowerSeller, 14

**L**
Limited liability corporation, 89
Liquidators, buying from, 31–32
Listing
 designer, 49

featured, 106
fixed price, 45
items, 37–60
   private, 45
   standard, 40
Local auctions, 34
Local computer shops, 6–7
Location, item, 48
Logistics, the, 17–26
Lots, selling, 47–48

**M**

Mac-fanatics, selling to, 14
Manufacturers, buying from, 29
Marketing
   e-mail, 107
   outside eBay, 108
   within eBay, 104–109
Marketplace Research service, 94–95
Materials, 91–92
mcpricebrakers, 16, 80, 83, 134
Money for small business, Microsoft's, 121
Money orders, 25
Multiple items, 47
My eBay page, 25–26
myob.com, 115

**N**

New items, sources for, 28–32
New markets for old hardware, 10

Newegg.com, 7–8
Newsletter, e-mail, 108
Newspaper advertising, 34–35, 109
Nicotera, Mark, PowerSeller, 13
No reserve auctions, 64–65, 67
notebooksauction-dot-com, 12, 74, 82, 135

**O**

One dollar, low reserve method, 62–64
One dollar, no reserve method, 64–65
Overture's marketing tools, 109

**P**

Page counter, 52
Partnership, 88
Payment
   instructions, 55
   methods, 24–25, 52–53
PayPal, 24–25
PeachTree business accounting software, 121
Peak auction hours, 46
Personal checks, 25
Personal loans, 87
Photo hosting services, 99–101
Photobucket.com, 100–101
Photographs, 73–74
Pictures, 73–74
   adding, 48–50

Post-auction, 79–80
PowerSellers
   bios of five eBay, 12–16
   closing thoughts from, 134–135
   qualifications of, 11
Powerselling vs. selling as a hobby, 2–3
powersourceonline.com, 31
Pre-auction customer consideration, 77–78
Pre-filling information, 40
Pricing, 61–67
   and duration, 43–46
Problems, 81–84
Profitability vs. risk, 67
Promoting your listing, 50
Promotional
   ideas, 107–108
   programs, 109

**Q**
Quantity, 47–48
Questions, customer, 78–79
QuickBooks business accounting program, 121

**R**
Registering for an account, 17–20
Research tools, 94–97
Reserve price, 43–44, 66–67
Retailers, 30–31

Return policy, 55
Review and submit, 55–56

**S**
S corporation, 89
Sales channel, using eBay as, 13
Sales tax, 55
Scams, beware of, 81–82
Scanner, 74
Scott, Benjamin, PowerSeller, 12
Selling Manager, 98
Selling Manager Pro, 98
Selling preferences, 23
Skype, 78–79
Shipping, 2, 91–92, 111–117
   companies, 117
   complaints, 83–84
   drop, 111–112
   location, 48
   options, 53–54
Sniping, 46
Sole proprietorship, 87–88
Solutions directory, eBay's, 93, 101
Somerset Capital Group, Ltd., 13
somersetsales, PowerSeller, 13, 67, 81, 105, 134
Specifics, item, 42
Start time, auction, 45
Start-up financing, 86–87
Starting a business, 85–92

Starting price, 43, 62
Storage, 90–91, 113–117
  facility layout, 115–117
Stores, eBay, 56–58
  cross-promotion through, 50, 59–60
  Referral Credit Program, 109
  setting up your, 58–59
  understanding the 24/7 commitment of, 60
Subcategories, 39–40
Subtitle, 41–42, 49
Success, what it takes, 1–2

**T**
Teaser auctions, 106
Tech-trickle-down, 9–10
Technological innovation, rapid pace of, 9–10
Terapeak.com, 95–96
Timing your auctions, 104–105
Title, 41, 70–71
  and description, 41–43
Tools to help you work smarter, 93–101
Trade magazine advertising, 109
Traffic times, peak, 46
Truition.com, 99
TurboLister, 98

**U**
U.S. Postal Service, 117
Up-selling, 59–60

UPS, 117
Used items, sources for, 32–35
User agreement and privacy policy, 18–20
User ID and password, 20

**V**
Vernon Technology Solutions, 15
VillagePhoto, 100
Visibility, increasing your item's, 49–50

**W**
Wal-Mart, 5
Warehouse, 115–117
Web site advertising, 109
When things go wrong, 81–84
Wholesalers, 30